Editorial Project Manager
Eric Migliaccio

Editor in Chief
Karen J. Goldfluss, M.S. Ed.

Creative Director
Sarah M. Fournier

Cover Artist
Diem Pascarella

Illustrator
Clint McKnight

Art Coordinator
Renée Mc Elwee

Imaging
Amanda R. Harter

Publisher
Mary D. Smith, M.S. Ed.

MASTERING COMPLEX TEXT

Grade 6

Using Multiple Reading Sources

TCR 8070

Includes:

- 25 Units with 3 – 5 related text sources in a variety of genres and formats
- Multiple question types that promote higher-order thinking skills
- Open-ended response opportunities to encourage close reading
- Correlated to the Common Core State Standards

Teacher Created Resources

Author
Karen McRae

W9-CIK-835

CORRELATED TO COMMON CORE STANDARDS

For correlations to the Common Core State Standards, see pages 109–112 of this book or visit *http://www.teachercreated.com/standards/*.

Teacher Created Resources
6421 Industry Way
Westminster, CA 92683
www.teachercreated.com

ISBN: 978-1-4206-8070-6

© 2015 Teacher Created Resources
Made in U.S.A.

Teacher Created Resources

Table of Contents

Introduction

Here we are, teaching and learning at the beginning of a new era of educational standards: the Common Core Era. This new directive has ushered in a slew of educational guidelines that are somewhat familiar and yet entirely ambitious. While the Common Core State Standards for English Language Arts address many educational basics (reading comprehension, proficiency in the conventions of English grammar, the ability to express oneself both in writing and in speech), they also seek to define what it means to be a literate, resourceful, perceptive person in the 21st century. Ultimately, they aim to equip each student with the tools needed to be that kind of person.

Introduction (cont.)

With this new, ambitious focus comes the need for a new type of educational material—one that challenges and interests students while meeting the multifaceted criteria of the Common Core. There are a total of 25 units in *Mastering Complex Text Using Multiple Reading Sources*, and each one fits the bill. Here's how:

✳ **The units in this book are both familiar and innovative.**

They are familiar in that they pair reading passages with activities that test reading comprehension. They are innovative in how they accomplish this goal through the use of multiple text sources and multiple answer formats. These materials promote deeper understanding and thought processes by prompting students to analyze, synthesize, hypothesize, and empathize.

✳ **The use of multiple reading sources promotes close reading.**

Close reading is the underlying goal of the Common Core State Standards for English Language Arts. Close reading involves understanding not just the explicit content of a reading passage but also all of the nuances contained therein. A close reading of a text reveals all of the inferential and structural components of the content, while also illuminating the craft that went into the writing of it.

The Common Core State Standards suggest that the best way to foster close reading of informational text is through text complexity. It offers four factors needed to create a high level of text complexity—all four of which are achieved through this book's use of multiple reading sources:

Factor	Meaning
1. Levels of Purpose	The purpose of the text should be implicit, hidden, or obscured in some way.
2. Structure	Texts of high complexity tend to have complex, implicit, or unconventional structures.
3. Language Conventionality or Clarity	Texts should use domain-specific language and feature language that is figurative, ironic, ambiguous, or otherwise unfamiliar.
4. Knowledge Demands	Complex texts make assumptions that readers can use life experiences, cultural awareness, and content knowledge to supplement their understanding of a text.

✳ **The activities prompt students to explore the reading material from all angles.**

By completing the four different activities found in each unit, students will be able to display a broad understanding of the reading material. Each activity and question is designed to make students think about what they have read—everything from how it was written, to why it was written that way, to how its subject matter can be applied to their lives. They gain experience locating information, making inferences from it, and applying knowledge in a variety of ways.

The units in this book are supplemented by a comprehensive answer key (pages 101–108) and a full list of Common Core State Standards correlations (pages 109–112). And even more educational value can be mined from each unit's reading material with "Additional Activities" (page 100). Make copies of this page (one per student per unit) and have students follow the instructions.

How to Use This Book

This book is divided into 25 units, which do not need to be taught in any particular order. Each unit is composed of reading material (one or two pages) and activity pages (two or three pages):

Reading Material

The reading material for each unit consists of three or four text sources. Have students read all of a unit's text sources before proceeding to the activity pages. These sources complement each other, and a connective thread (or threads) runs throughout them. Sometimes these connections will be explicit, while at other times they will be hidden or obscured.

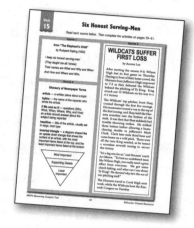

❋ Another Approach After reading the source material, ask students to name all of the ways in which the reading sources seem to be related or connected. See page 100 for more details.

Activity Pages

Each unit is supported by two or three pages of activities. These activity pages are divided into four parts:

Part 1

The Common Core asks students to draw on information from multiple print sources and show the ability to locate an answer to a question quickly or to solve a problem efficiently. This section directly correlates to that standard. Students will gain valuable practice in scanning multiple text sources in order to locate information.

Before beginning this section, remind students to read the directions carefully. Some of the information can be found in two or more sources, which means that students will need to fill in more than one bubble in those instances.

❋ Another Approach Have your students practice their recognition of genres and formats. For each unit, have them fill in the chart on page 100.

Part 2

In this section, students are asked to provide the best answer(s) to multiple-choice questions. What sets these apart from the usual multiple-choice questions is their emphasis on higher-order thinking skills. Very few questions ask for simple recall of information. Instead, these questions are designed to provide practice and strengthen knowledge in a variety of areas, including the following:

- ❋ inference
- ❋ deduction
- ❋ grammar and usage
- ❋ vocabulary in context
- ❋ word etymology
- ❋ parts of speech
- ❋ literary devices
- ❋ authorial intent
- ❋ compare and contrast
- ❋ cause and effect
- ❋ analogies
- ❋ computation

❋ Another Approach Ask each student to write an original multiple-choice question based on the reading sources. Use the best or most interesting questions to create a student-generated quiz. See page 100 for more details.

How to Use This Book (cont.)

Activity Pages (cont.)

Part 3

This two-question section takes the skills addressed in Part 1 and approaches them from another angle. Part 3 is in the form of a scavenger hunt that asks students to search the sources in order to locate a word or phrase that fits the criteria described. Students are also asked to name the source in which they found the word or phrase.

> ❋ **Another Approach** Assign students to small groups, and have each group collaboratively come up with two suitable scavenger hunts from the reading material. These student-created scavenger hunts can then be completed and discussed by the entire class. See page 100 for more details.

Part 4

This section is composed of three questions that ask students to integrate information from several texts on the same topic in order to write knowledgeably about a subject. The vast majority of these questions are open-ended, while the rest involve using a new format (e.g., chart, diagram, graph) to organize and/or interpret data and information.

The questions in this section challenge students to blend close-reading concepts with flexible-thinking skills. Students are asked to do the following:

Analyze	Synthesize	Hypothesize	Empathize
❋ authorial choices ❋ intent of characters/ historical figures ❋ overall meanings ❋ quotations in context ❋ statistical data	❋ combine different takes on the same subject ❋ use information from different genres and formats (nonfiction, fiction, graphs, etc.) to draw conclusions ❋ compare and contrast characters, ideas, and concepts ❋ draw conclusions from information and/or numerical data	❋ make predictions about future events ❋ explore alternatives to previous choices	❋ connect to one's own life ❋ put oneself in a character's/ historical figure's place

> ❋ **Another Approach** The Common Core places a strong emphasis on teaching and applying speaking and listening skills. Many of the questions in Part 4 lend themselves well to meeting standards from this strand. Have individual students present oral reports on specific Part 4 questions. Or, form groups of students and ask them to engage in collaborative discussion before presenting their findings.

Creating a Stir

Read each source below. Then complete the activities on pages 7–8.

Source 1

Figurative language describes something by comparing it with something else.

* ✳ **simile** (a comparison using *like* or *as*) — The car was <u>as slow as a snail</u>.

* ✳ **onomatopoeia** (the use of a word to imitate a sound) — The truck's loud <u>boom</u> woke him from his slumber.

* ✳ **idiom** (a common phrase whose total meaning is different from the meaning of the individual words) — The president <u>created a stir</u> when he signed the controversial bill.

(**Note:** The antonym of *figurative* is *literal*.)

Source 2

Vote **YES** on Free, Clean Power!

For too long, we have relied on fossil fuels like oil to light and heat our homes. These fuels pollute our air, land, and water; and what's more, they won't be around forever. Once they're gone, they're not coming back.

This is why wind energy is so important. Wind energy is clean. That means that it doesn't produce pollution. No chemicals are required to tap into this power. Our environment will stay protected.

Look around you. Wind is everywhere. It's free, and it can never be used up! We can harness this natural power and use it forever. Using the power of wind will ensure that we don't have to buy oil and other fossil fuels from other countries. This will give us financial freedom by keeping our money in our country.

By voting **YES** on September 2, you can make a dream of clean energy come true. Beautiful wind farms will be built immediately. The whispering whir of the windmills will soon signal a new era of energy efficiency. Opponents of this law will say that these wind farms will cost too much to build, but that cost will be more than paid for within a few short years.

Can you feel the winds of change stirring? The time is now to begin looking to a new future with cleaner, more renewable energy. The time is now to vote **YES**.

Source 3

Vote **NO** on these noisy nuisances!

Rumble! Scrape! Clang! Don't let anyone fool you: windmills cause pollution . . . noise pollution! When the large, mechanical parts in windmills are turning and stirring the air, there can be no peace and quiet. It's like living inside a washing machine. The noises are loud and disturbing, and they are nearly constant. You can't escape them. Is that what you want in your ears and in your home 24/7?

Wind energy is not some magical solution that will solve all of our energy problems. Sure, wind is free, but building wind farms is the furthest thing from free. It will cost millions of our hard-earned tax dollars. Also, the wind doesn't always blow. It's inconsistent. We need energy that is reliable and always available at the flick of a switch. If we become dependent on the weather for our energy, we will lose some of the freedom we have worked so hard for.

Our opponents want you to think that wind farms only help the environment. Ask the birds if that's true! Windmills' sharp blades are dangerous to the local wildlife. Windmills also require a lot of open space. Should we cut down trees to make room for them? Many animals make their homes in those trees.

Lastly, wind farms are unattractive. They do not blend in with the natural landscape of our town. They will stick out like a sore thumb.

Vote **NO** this September 2!

Creating a Stir *(cont.)*

Name: _____

Part 1: Read each idea. Which source gives you this information? Fill in the correct bubble for each source. (Note: More than one bubble may be filled in for each idea.)

Information	Sources ➡	1	2	3
1. Oil is a fossil fuel.		◯	◯	◯
2. Windmills create wind energy.		◯	◯	◯
3. Wind is a renewable form of energy.		◯	◯	◯
4. The vote will take place on September 2.		◯	◯	◯

Part 2: Fill in the bubble(s) next to the best answer(s) to each question.

5. Which aspects of the wind-energy debate are mentioned by both the YES and NO sides?

   Ⓐ how fossil fuels pollute   Ⓒ how windmills sound

   Ⓑ how windmills look   Ⓓ from whom we buy oil

6. Which of the following terms describe the underlined phrase in this sentence: I was so tired, I <u>hit the hay</u> around 8:00 last night.

   Ⓐ simile   Ⓒ literal language

   Ⓑ idiom   Ⓓ figurative language

7. Which of these words means "unable to do without"?

   Ⓐ dependent   Ⓒ constant

   Ⓑ independent   Ⓓ inconsistent

8. In Source 3, to what does "24/7" refer?

   Ⓐ how loud the sound of windmills is

   Ⓑ how constant the sound of windmills is

   Ⓒ how expensive the building of wind farms is

   Ⓓ how many "NO" votes it will take to win

Part 3: Search Sources 2 and 3 of "Creating a Stir" to find **one** example of each of the following. Then write the number of the source in which you located this information.

9. onomatopoeia _____   Source #: _____

10. simile _____   Source #: _____

_____

Name: _____

Part 4: Refer back to the sources, and use complete sentences to answer these questions.

11. *Alliteration* is the repetition of beginning sounds (example, Peter picked a peck of pickled peppers). Search Sources 2 and 3 to find a sentence that contains more than one example of alliteration. Use quotation marks and write that sentence in the box below.

12. Think about how the authors in Sources 2 and 3 use reasons and evidence to make their case for or against wind energy. In each empty box in the chart below, summarize the reasons each author gives for his/her opinion.

	Source 2	**Source 3**
Pollution		
Cost		
Freedom		

13. Name two ways in which the windmills in "Creating a Stir" are creating a stir. One way should be figurative, while the other is literal.

_____

_____

_____

_____

_____

_____

Falling Off and Growing In

Read each source below. Then complete the activities on pages 10–11.

Source 1

deciduous (deh-si-dyoo-us)
adjective

means "tending to fall off"; describes something that falls off or is shed during a certain time of year or at a certain stage of development

Examples:

- Deciduous trees shed their leaves in the winter.
- Humans shed their deciduous teeth during childhood.

Source 2

On the screen at the front of the class was a picture showing two trees. Mr. Oakley pointed at them as he spoke. "Today, we are going to learn about the two main categories of trees: **coniferous** and **deciduous**. Let's first look at the tree on the left. It is a coniferous tree. Coniferous trees are often called evergreen trees, and they tend to grow upward more so than outward. This often gives them a triangular shape, like a Christmas tree. This shape makes evergreen trees strong, and it helps them to support the weight of snow. Instead of leaves, coniferous trees usually have long, pointed needles. These needles stay on the tree throughout the winter and other seasons."

Mr. Oakley then pointed to the tree on the right. Its branches were more spread out and covered with broad leaves. "By contrast, take a look at a deciduous tree. Maples, oaks, and hickories are some common types of deciduous trees. These trees tend to grow outward, and they have leaves that fall off when winter hits. In fact, that's how they get their name. The word *deciduous* means 'tending to fall off'. These trees lose their leaves as a means of survival during the winter. Much like an animal going into hibernation for the winter, a deciduous tree becomes dormant. It slows down the way it takes in and uses nutrients. Then, when spring comes around again, the tree becomes active again and its leaves begin to grow."

Source 3

The whole house is in an uproar. My little sister lost a tooth. It came right out when she bit into an apple. She's freaking out, saying she'll never again be able to smile for pictures. My dad is trying to calmly tell her about baby teeth (which he calls "primary teeth" and some other big word I can't remember). He's giving her a whole story about how she has 20 baby teeth (well, 19 now) but soon she'll have 28 permanent teeth just like I do. Then he mumbled something about him and Mom having 32 teeth. (My dad's explanations are usually complicated.)

Phoebe isn't buying it. It doesn't matter how calmly you explain things to my sister, she gets hysterical when things like this happen. I even offered to help. (I was in a generous mood, I guess.) I told her that losing a baby tooth isn't so bad. You actually *get paid* for it. I could tell her from experience that the whole "tooth fairy" situation is a pretty good deal, and she should enjoy it while it lasts. I could also tell her that it's just part of growing up, but I don't think that would make her feel any better.

Source 4

Development of Teeth in Humans

	Number	Emerge	Fall Out
Primary Teeth	20	6 months–3 years	6 years–12 years
Permanent Teeth	32	6 years–21 years*	

* The first 28 permanent teeth usually emerge by age 13. The final four—they're often called the wisdom teeth—don't emerge until ages 17–21.

Name: _____

Part 1: Read each idea. Which source gives you this information? Fill in the correct bubble for each source. (Note: More than one bubble may be filled in for each idea.)

Information	Sources ➡	1	2	3	4
1. Adult humans have up to 32 permanent teeth.		○	○	○	○
2. Young children have fewer than 32 teeth.		○	○	○	○
3. Deciduous trees lose their leaves in the winter.		○	○	○	○
4. Evergreen trees do not shed seasonally.		○	○	○	○

Part 2: Fill in the bubble next to the best answer to each question.

5. Based on the information given in Source 2, which word would be a synonym for *dormant*?

Ⓐ falling

Ⓒ permanent

Ⓑ inactive

Ⓓ broad

6. Some of the writing in Source 3 provides facts about the events occurring in the story, while some expresses the narrator's opinion or impression of events. Which of the following quotes does both?

Ⓐ "The whole house is in an uproar."

Ⓑ "My little sister lost a tooth."

Ⓒ "It came right out when she bit into an apple."

Ⓓ "She's freaking out, saying she'll never again be able to smile for pictures."

7. Complete this analogy: **deciduous** are to **leaves** as **coniferous** are to _____.

Ⓐ evergreen

Ⓒ needles

Ⓑ winter

Ⓓ permanent

8. Complete this analogy: **leaf** is to **leaves** as **tooth** is to _____.

Ⓐ teeth

Ⓒ emerge

Ⓑ primary

Ⓓ fall out

Part 3: Search "Falling Off and Growing In" to find words with the following meanings. Then write the number of the source in which you located this information.

9. "a loud disturbance" _____ Source #: _____

10. "to move out and come into view" _____ Source #: _____

Name: _____

Part 4: Refer back to the sources, and use complete sentences to answer these questions.

11. In the space below, draw a sketch of the picture that Mr. Oakley shows his class in Source 2. Use the clues given to make the sketch as accurate as possible. Label each object in the picture.

12. About how old is the narrator of Source 3? Use specific clues given in Sources 3 and 4 to make an informed guess. Then explain your reasoning below.

_____

_____

_____

_____

_____

_____

_____

13. Give two other terms for "baby teeth," and explain how you know these terms. (**Hint:** One is mentioned directly in the sources, and the other can be inferred from the information given.)

_____

_____

_____

_____

_____

_____

_____

The Dynamic Trio

Read each source below and on page 13. Then complete the activities on pages 14–15.

1. (as **adjective**) energetic, forceful

   Dana's <u>dynamic</u> personality made her one of the leaders of our group.

2. (as **noun**) the way that two or more people behave with each other

   Having fun and making jokes was a big part of our group's <u>dynamic</u>.

Silver Screen Cinema
"Where movies come to life!"

Theater 1 • The Dynamic Trio
Three unlikely partners—a 4-year-old and two rival superheroes—join forces to battle bad guys.
Running Time: 102 minutes
Showtimes for Saturday, March 28: 10:30   12:25   2:20   4:15   6:10   8:05

Theater 2 • The Tails of Two Kitties
Two mischievous kittens vie for the attention of a famous French actress.
Running Time: 99 minutes
Showtimes for Saturday, March 28: 10:20   12:20   2:20   4:20   6:20   8:20

Theater 3 • Old Hat
An aging wizard must change his ways in order to match wits with a new enemy.
Running Time: 123 minutes
Showtimes for Saturday, March 28: 11:50   2:10   4:30   6:50   9:10

Theater 4 • Space Neighbors II
A new crew of aliens explores Earth in this long-awaited follow-up to *Space Neighbors*.
Running Time: 96 minutes
Showtimes for Saturday, March 28: 2:20   4:05   5:50   7:35   9:20   11:00

Theater 5 • The History of Sound
Five talented musicians form a band and learn to work together to succeed.
Running Time: 202 minutes
Showtimes for Saturday, March 28: 10:40   2:35   6:30   10:15

Theater 6 • Only Game in Town
A mysterious inventor designs a new board game that makes the world a better place.
Running Time: 114 minutes
Showtimes for Saturday, March 28: 12:25   2:45   5:05   7:25   9:45

Theater 7 • The Best-Kept Secret
A shocking discovery has scientists racing against the clock to solve an ancient riddle.
Running Time: 130 minutes
Showtimes for Saturday, March 28: 12:10   2:40   5:10   7:40   10:10

Source 3

Number Words

The following words are used to describe a certain number of things, people, ideas, etc.

duo → two			**sextet** → six	
trio → three			**septet** → seven	
quartet → four			**octet** → eight	
quintet → five				

Source 4

"What should we see on Saturday night?" asked Carmen. "There must something good playing at Silver Screen Cinema that night."

"I don't know about that," said Carl. "I find that most of the films they show there are dreadful."

Ignoring Carl's comment, Rico said, "First, let's find out when the movies are playing and determine what time would work for us. I can't meet up with you two until after 6:00 that night."

"And I have to be home by 10:00 p.m.," volunteered Carmen. "Sorry!"

"I'm available at any time," said Carl.

As he accessed the theater's website on his smartphone, Rico said, "The good news is that this theater starts its movies right on time. That's important to know, because we should probably factor in about 20 minutes after the movie to discuss what we liked about it."

"Or didn't like," added Carl quickly.

Still looking at his phone, Rico said, "Of the movies playing at Silver Screen Cinema, I'll watch anything but *Old Hat*. I saw that last week with my parents."

"Cross that one off the list," agreed Carl. "As for me, I would prefer to not sit through a silly science-fiction sequel or a movie about kids or animals. Generally, those types of films are for less sophisticated viewers. I am intrigued by *The History of Sound*. I read a review that said it is quite good."

"It's also over three hours long!" laughed Carmen. "But if that's the one we all agree on, then I'm game."

"Alright," said Rico as he scanned the theater's website. "Looking over the showtimes and considering everybody's criteria, I think there's only one movie we can all agree on that fits into our time schedule." He angled his phone so that Carmen and Carl could clearly see the title of the movie he was referring to. They nodded their heads and said, "Let's see it!"

The Dynamic Trio *(cont.)*

Name: _____

Part 1: Read each idea. Which source gives you this information? Fill in the correct bubble for each source. (Note: More than one bubble may be filled in for each idea.)

Information	Sources ➡	1	2	3	4
1. *Old Hat* is a movie playing at Silver Screen Cinema.		○	○	○	○
2. *The History of Sound* is over 3 hours long.		○	○	○	○
3. *The Dynamic Trio* is playing at Silver Screen Cinema.		○	○	○	○
4. A trio consists of three people.		○	○	○	○

Part 2: Fill in the bubble next to the best answer to each question.

5. "Running Time" tells you how long a movie is. How many of the films in Source 2 are under two hours in length?

Ⓐ 3 　　　　　Ⓑ 4 　　　　　Ⓒ 5 　　　　　Ⓓ 6

6. Which words (in order) would be used to fill in the blanks of this statement: Source 2 describes a _____ of films, while Source 3 defines a _____ of words.

Ⓐ septet, octet 　　　　　　　　Ⓒ sextet, septet

Ⓑ septet, sextet 　　　　　　　　Ⓓ septet, septet

7. The unit is titled "The Dynamic Trio." To what does this title most likely refer?

Ⓐ the definitions of *dynamic* given in Source 1

Ⓑ the definition of words given in Source 3

Ⓒ the characters described in Source 4

Ⓓ the title of the movie the characters in Source 4 agree to see

8. Which film in Source 2 is about the dynamic between a quintet of performers?

Ⓐ *The Tails of Two Kitties* 　　　　　Ⓒ *The History of Sound*

Ⓑ *Space Neighbors II* 　　　　　　　Ⓓ *The Best-Kept Secret*

Part 3: Search "The Dynamic Trio" to find one example of each of the following. Then write the number of the source in which you located this information.

9. an 8-letter adjective meaning "terrible" _____ 　 Source #: _____

10. a 3-letter verb meaning "compete" _____ 　 Source #: _____

Part 4: Refer back to the sources, and use complete sentences to answer these questions.

11. In the conversation from Source 4, what is the dynamic between these three people? How does each member of the group behave?

_____

_____

_____

_____

_____

_____

_____

12. In Source 4, each person has schedules and preferences that affect which movie the group can see together. For each person, write down each of these. The first one is done for you.

Carmen	Carl	Rico
must be home by 10:00 p.m.		

13. Taking into account all of the clues given in Source 4 and all of the movies listed in Source 2, which one do the three friends agree to see? Fill out this information on the ticket stub below.

Theater Number

Title of Movie

Showtime

#Symbols

Read each source below. Then complete the activities on pages 17–18.

Source 1

"Stop that thief! He is stealing money."   "How does she know that?"

Source 2

The **#** symbol has the following meanings:

- **number sign**—This symbol is used to designate a number ("#2" can be read as "number two").

- **pound sign**—In the United States, the # sign on a telephone keypad is often called the "pound sign." In the United Kingdom, it is never referred to in this way. The term "pound sign" is only used when referring to the symbol for pound sterling, which is a form of English currency (money). The symbol for this currency looks like this: £.

- **hash sign**—In many countries, the # symbol is called a hash sign. In the 2010s, this symbol has seen an increase in usage due to social media on the Internet. In this context, the hash sign is used in front of a topic. Together, the symbol and the topic are referred to as a "hashtag" (for example, "#money" is read as "hashtag money").

Note: The # sign should not be confused with the sharp sign (♯) in musical notation. The horizontal lines on the sharp sign slant upward from left to right, unlike those on the number sign.

Source 3

Dear "Pete":

I am shocked and appalled! I recently purchased a product called Bug Be Gone from Pete's Pest Control. This product contains a large skull-and-crossbones symbol (☠) on the back of the can. I am aware that this symbol has long been used to show that something contains poison. Times change, however, and I feel that the use of this symbol on the outside of the container is now more dangerous than the chemicals found inside the container.

Now more than ever, children love pirates. My niece and nephew are big fans of a very popular TV show about a congenial pirate. They also love to play "Pirates." They pretend their bunk bed is a pirate ship, and they decorate flags to hang from the bed. Can you guess what symbol they draw on their pirate flags? That's right, they draw the skull-and-crossbones symbol, which has been used by pirates since the 1700s. Young children associate this symbol with fun games and colorful characters.

I am dismayed to think this symbol may draw young children to your toxic product. Please act immediately to alter this product's label or remove it entirely from your shelves. Any other course of action would be irresponsible.

Sincerely,
A concerned aunt

Name: _____

Part 1: Read each idea. Which source gives you this information? Fill in the correct bubble for each source. (Note: More than one bubble may be filled in for each idea.)

Information	Sources ➡	1	2	3
1. Some symbols can have more than one meaning.		○	○	○
2. The # symbol can be used in front of a number.		○	○	○
3. The # symbol can be used in front of a topic.		○	○	○
4. The ♯ symbol can stand for the word "sharp."		○	○	○

Part 2: Fill in the bubble next to the best answer to each question.

5. What is a synonym for the word *sharp* as it is used in Source 1?

   Ⓐ high-pitched   Ⓒ flat

   Ⓑ low-pitched   Ⓓ intelligent

6. If the same cartoon that appears in Source 1 were being created for an audience from the United Kingdom, which symbol would most likely be drawn on the bag?

   Ⓐ ☠   Ⓒ £

   Ⓑ ♯   Ⓓ $

7. Which of these words from Source 3 has a positive connotation?

   Ⓐ appalled   Ⓒ congenial

   Ⓑ dismayed   Ⓓ toxic

8. What is a synonym for the word *draw* as it is used in the final paragraph of Source 3?

   Ⓐ illustrate   Ⓒ show

   Ⓑ attract   Ⓓ display

Part 3: Search "#Symbols" to find one example of each of the following. Then write the number of the source in which you located this information.

9. a contraction _____   Source #: _____

10. the name of a century _____   Source #: _____

Name: _____

Part 4: Refer back to the sources, and use complete sentences to answer these questions.

11. Name some pros (positives) and some cons (negatives) to using symbols in place of words. Use examples from the sources to make your case for each side of the argument.

_____

_____

_____

_____

_____

_____

_____

_____

12. You work at Pete's Pest Control, and it is your job to read the mail and inform Pete (the owner) about any issues. Pete feels he is too busy to read a whole letter, and he only wants to know the "important parts." In the box below, write a brief summary of the letter in Source 3 and explain the customer's concerns.

13. Do you agree or disagree with the author of Source 3 when she claims that a symbol on a container can be more dangerous than the poison inside the container? Explain your answer.

_____

_____

_____

_____

_____

_____

_____

The Prototype

Read each source below. Then complete the activities on pages 20–21.

Source 1

On This Day in History

Date: **December 1, 1913**

Event: Henry Ford installs the first moving assembly line and uses it to build Model T automobiles quickly and cheaply.

Summary: Ford didn't invent the assembly line, but he was the first to use it in this way and for the building of this much product. He divided the assembly of each Model T into 84 steps. A different worker was in charge of each step. The workers never moved. Instead, a conveyor belt brought the unfinished automobile to them. As the vehicle moved along the line, it gained parts until it was completed by the 84th step. Using this method, it took only $2\frac{1}{2}$ hours to build a complete Model T. This efficient use of time and workers allowed Ford to sell his cars for a price that many people could afford. From 1913–1927, Ford sold millions of Model T cars. His moving assembly lines became the prototype on which other companies modeled their production.

Source 2

Glossary of Terms

assembly line — an arrangement of workers and machines at various stations with the purpose of assembling a complex machine

entrepreneur (on-treh-preh-nur) — a person who starts a business

overhead — the fixed cost (for example, rent, lighting, heating, machinery) of running a business

profit — the leftover money a business makes after the cost of producing products and paying employees

prototype — the model of something, from which other things are copied or further developed

trademark (™) — a symbol legally registered to represent a company or product

Source 3

Shapes Lee™

Let Lee help your child learn about shapes!

Each body part on this great new toy is a detachable shape made from cushiony, machine-washable material.

Source 4

Dear Mom and Pops,

The Shapes Lee™ doll is almost ready to take the world by storm! I've perfected a prototype, which will serve as a model that we can use to make millions of dolls. I've purchased enough parts to last a month, and I've assembled a great team of workers. I've even created an advertisement to get everyone excited about the product. All I need is a workspace. Is your garage available?

Here's my plan: I'll set up a 15-foot table with six workstations in your garage. One worker will stand at each station along the table. The first person (Gary) will attach the head onto the body and pass this along to the second person (Lucy). She'll attach the face onto the head. The third person (Kerry) adds the arms, and then the fourth person (Keith) adds the legs. Stan adds the hat, and puts the product into a box. I put each box into a larger box, to which I'll add shipping labels.

I'm convinced that this assembly-line method will allow us to produce hundreds of dolls (and thousands of dollars!) each day. And by using your garage, I can keep my overhead really low, and you know what that means! Soon I'll have enough money to afford my own apartment. You two deserve some peace and quiet after raising Katy and me. What do you say?

Your favorite entrepreneur,

Leeland Lewis

Name: _____

Part 1: Read each idea. Which source gives you this information? Fill in the correct bubble for each source. (Note: More than one bubble may be filled in for each idea.)

Information	Sources ➡	1	2	3	4
1. An assembly line can be used to build things.		O	O	O	O
2. Leeland is an entrepreneur who wants to make shape dolls.		O	O	O	O
3. The Shapes Lee™ doll wears a hat.		O	O	O	O
4. The Shapes Lee™ doll wears a triangular hat.		O	O	O	O

Part 2: Fill in the bubble(s) next to the best answer(s) to each question.

5. Who is not a part of Lee's assembly-line team?

    Ⓐ Katy   Ⓒ Keith

    Ⓑ Kerry   Ⓓ Leeland

6. What shape will Lucy be adding onto the doll at her workstation?

    Ⓐ circle   Ⓒ pentagon

    Ⓑ square   Ⓓ triangle

7. In Lee's plan to use his parents' garage, what is the average amount of workspace (in feet) each worker will have at the table? (**Hint:** The answer is reduced to lowest terms.)

    Ⓐ 2 feet   Ⓒ $6\frac{2}{5}$ feet

    Ⓑ $2\frac{1}{2}$ feet   Ⓓ 15 feet

8. Which of the following words from Source 2 are compound words?

    Ⓐ entrepreneur   Ⓒ profit

    Ⓑ overhead   Ⓓ trademark

Part 3: Search "The Prototype" to find words with the following meanings. (**Hint:** The number of syllables in the word is given in parentheses.) Then write the number of the source in which you located this information.

9. "soft and comfortable" (3 syllables) _____ Source #: _____

10. "easily removed" (4 syllables) _____ Source #: _____

The Prototype *(cont.)*

Name: _____

Part 4: Refer back to the sources to answer these questions.

11. What will the Shapes Lee doll look like at the end of each step on the assembly line? Write each worker's name in each station. Then draw sketches in the boxes below to show the doll being constructed in the way described by Lee in his letter.

Station 1	Station 2	Station 3	Station 4	Station 5	Station 6

12. Before Ford's factory began using the moving assembly line, they needed 12 hours to build a Model T. Use the graphic below to show how much more efficient the new process was. For each length of time it took Ford's factory to build one car using the new method, draw one car. Then fill in the blanks to answer the questions below.

Hours ➡	1	2	3	4	5	6	7	8	9	10	11	12

Using the new method, Ford's factory built _____ complete Model T cars in 12 hours. This left

_____number_____

them with _____ hours left over to begin building a _____ car.

_____number_____   _____ordinal number (like "1st")_____

13. Pretend that the Shapes Lee doll became a huge hit and millions were sold. Write a "This Day in History" entry for the Shapes Lee doll. Make up a date and a story to go with the huge success of this doll. Use at least three of the terms listed in Source 2.

On This Day in History

Date: _____

Event: _____

Summary: _____

_____

_____

_____

A Little from a Lot

Read each source below and on page 23. Then complete the activities on pages 24–25.

Source 1

 **infographic** — a graphic representation of data and knowledge designed to present a lot of information quickly, clearly, and in a way that is visually appealing

---

Source 2

It's Time to Make *A Go Of It* . . . @ Agoofit.com

"Get what you need from the world by giving the world what it needs."™

Do you have a great idea? Are you ready to change the world for the better? Use our website to get your idea up and running. It's called **crowdfunding**, and here's how it works:

You have an idea.

You register at *Agoofit.com*.*

You ask for small donations.

You incentivize your offer.

Millions of people visit *Agoofit.com*.

Many like your idea and want to donate a few dollars.

All of those small donations add up.**

Your dream becomes a reality!

---

* A $25 fee is due upon registration to *Agoofit.com*.   ** 20% of all donations received go to *Agoofit.com*.

Source 3

| portmanteau | a word created by fusing together the sounds and meanings of two or more words |

Examples: brunch (*breakfast* and *lunch*); spork (*spoon* and *fork*); infographic (*information* and *graphic*)

Source 4

Inventive. Innovative. Inspired.

These three words best describe Leeland Learning, a company dedicated to creating fantabulous products that instruct and delight little learners. Our newest product is the Shapes Lee™ doll.

Each body part on this great toy is a detachable shape made from cushiony, machine-washable material. Best of all,

Shapes Lee™ puts a friendly face on learning.™

Leeland Learning is ready to produce a large quantity of these dolls in time for the upcoming holiday season, but we need your help. A state-of-the-art warehouse is needed to assemble dolls and process orders.

Please help us help the children.

Money Goal: $100,000 (This is just a guesstimate of how much funds will be needed.)

> **We Offer the Following Incentives:**
>
> Level 1: Those who contribute $10 will receive a free download of the Shapes Lee™ theme song.
>
> Level 2: Those who contribute $25 will receive their very own Shapes Lee™ doll.
>
> Level 3: Those who contribute $75 will receive all previous awards, plus a visit from our Shapes Lee™ mascot.
>
> Level 4: Those who contribute $1,000 will receive all previous awards, plus have their picture permanently displayed on our website.

Sincerely,
Leeland Lewis

CEO Leeland Learning

This crowdfunding campaign is sponsored by Agoofit.com.

A Little from a Lot (cont.)

Name: _____

Part 1: Refer back to Source 4 to answer each math question about Leeland Learning's crowdfunding campaign.

1. How many Level 1 donations are needed to reach the money goal? _____

2. How many Level 2 donations are needed to reach the money goal? _____

3. How many Level 4 donations are needed to reach the money goal? _____

4. If the goal is reached, how much money would *Agoofit.com* keep? _____

Part 2: Fill in the bubble(s) next to the best answer(s) to each question.

5. Which of the following is a visual representation of an inventive idea?

Ⓐ　　　　　Ⓑ　　　　　Ⓒ　　　　　Ⓓ

6. Which of these words from the sources is a compound word (and not a portmanteau word)?

　Ⓐ infographic　　　　　Ⓒ crowdfunding

　Ⓑ detachable　　　　　Ⓓ state-of-the-art

7. Which of these words from the sources means "offer a reward for doing something"?

　Ⓐ assemble　　　　　Ⓒ process

　Ⓑ incentivize　　　　　Ⓓ produce

8. What are two things that *Agoofit.com* and Leeland Learning have in common?

　Ⓐ They are both named after portmanteau words.

　Ⓑ They both have websites.

　Ⓒ They both have slogans.

　Ⓓ They both create and sell learning products.

Part 3: Search "A Little from a Lot" to find one example of each of the following. Then write the number of the source in which you located this information.

9. a portmanteau meaning "give a possible answer" _____ Source #: _____

10. a portmanteau meaning "really terrific" _____ Source #: _____

Name: _____

Part 4: Refer back to the sources, and use complete sentences to answer these questions.

11. The title of this unit ("A Little from a Lot") best describes which of these things? (Fill in the circle of the correct answer, and then explain your answer on the lines below.)

Ⓐ portmanteaus   Ⓑ infographics   Ⓒ crowdfunding

_____

_____

_____

_____

12. Source 2 uses an infographic to explain the concept of crowdfunding. Take the information given in Source 2 and rewrite it in your own words as a short paragraph.

_____

_____

_____

_____

_____

13. The boxed portion of Source 4 is in the form of a list. Use this information to create an infographic.

A Fit for Her Environment

Read each source below. Then complete the activities on pages 27–28.

Source 1

"It's so hot," Ann groaned and tugged at her T-shirt. The black fabric clung to her sweaty back.

Ann's mom shook her head. "I told you to wear white for our hike in the desert."

"But my black shirt is the *coolest*," said Ann.

Her mom laughed. "That's ironic, because it's just about the worst thing you could have worn to stay cool on such a hot day."

"White shirts are boring," said Ann.

"Maybe, but white is very good at reflecting heat and light away from your body. Black, on the other hand, absorbs the most light and heat from the sun. It attracts light and heat. That's why ballplayers put black paint under their eyes. They are trying to attract the sun to the black paint *under* their eyes, so it doesn't get *in* their eyes."

Ann fanned herself and squinted.

"Think of it this way," her mother continued, "black really soaks in heat and light. So your shirt—while very fashionable—is drenched in the hot light of the sun. Not really that *cool*, is it?"

Source 2

grasslands (noun) — a large open area of country covered with grass and low shrubs. Often used by animals for grazing. Usually found in climates that have distinct seasons (for example, hot summers).

Source 3

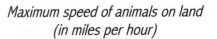

Maximum speed of animals on land (in miles per hour)

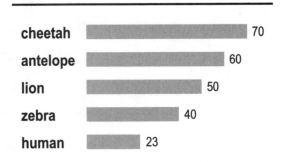

Animal	Speed
cheetah	70
antelope	60
lion	50
zebra	40
human	23

Source 4

Carla cleared her throat and began her report. "Cheetahs are especially good at two things: 1. sprinting, and 2. hunting animals like antelopes and zebras. I say 'sprinting' because cheetahs cannot run for long periods of time. But when they do run, wow! These cats are fast!"

Carla pressed a button, and a picture of a cheetah appeared on the screen behind her. Some of its body parts were labeled.

"A cheetah has a light, lean body and a long tail. Inside a cheetah's deep chest is a big heart and a set of extra-large lungs. These enlarged organs, along with its extra-wide nostrils, help the cheetah breathe in and use oxygen very well."

She continued, "While we're looking at the cheetah's face, notice the black lines that run from the corner of its eyes down to its mouth. These are called 'tear marks'. They help the cheetah see long distances across the sunny grasslands where it lives."

Carla paused to look at her notes. Then she started telling her classmates about the cheetah's amazing ground-gripping claws.

Name: _____

Part 1: Read each idea. Which source gives you this information? Fill in the correct bubble for each source. (Note: More than one bubble may be filled in for each idea.)

Information	Sources ➡	1	2	3	4
1. Cheetahs are fast runners.		○	○	○	○
2. Cheetahs can run about 30 mph faster than zebras.		○	○	○	○
3. White reflects more light than does black.		○	○	○	○
4. Grasslands often feature wide-open spaces.		○	○	○	○

Part 2: Fill in the bubble next to the best answer to each question.

5. Which piece of writing would be the most likely to come from a dictionary?

Ⓐ Source 1   Ⓑ Source 2   Ⓒ Source 3   Ⓓ Source 4

6. Who does the title "A Fit for Her Environment" best describe?

Ⓐ Ann   Ⓑ Ann's mom   Ⓒ Carla   Ⓓ a cheetah

7. Which of these statements about Source 4 is most true?

Ⓐ It is nonfiction, so all of the facts presented in it must be true.

Ⓑ It is nonfiction, but none of the facts presented in it can be true.

Ⓒ It is fiction, so none of the facts presented in it can be true.

Ⓓ It is fiction, but the facts presented in it could be true.

8. Imagine you are reading a story that contains this metaphor: "Uncle Joe was a cheetah, racing to the kitchen to grab the last cookie." Does this metaphor make sense? Why or why not?

Ⓐ No, Uncle Joe cannot run as fast as a cheetah.

Ⓑ Yes, Uncle Joe quickly pounced on food like a cheetah would.

Ⓒ No, cheetahs do not eat cookies.

Ⓓ Yes, Uncle Joe has large lungs and ground-gripping claws.

Part 3: Search "A Fit for Her Environment" to find one example of each of the following. Then write the number of the source in which you located this information.

9. a synonym for *soaked* _____ Source #: _____

10. an antonym for *shrunken* _____ Source #: _____

A Fit for Her Environment *(cont.)*

Name: ______________________________

Part 4: Refer back to the sources, and use complete sentences to answer these questions.

11. Something is ironic if it happens in the opposite way that one would expect it to. Why is it ironic when Ann says that her black shirt is "the coolest"?

____

____

____

____

12. On the picture below, show where the ballplayer would wear black paint in order to help him see the ball on a sunny day. Then, on the lines, explain how a cheetah's tear marks serve a purpose similar to the player's black paint.

____

____

____

____

____

____

____

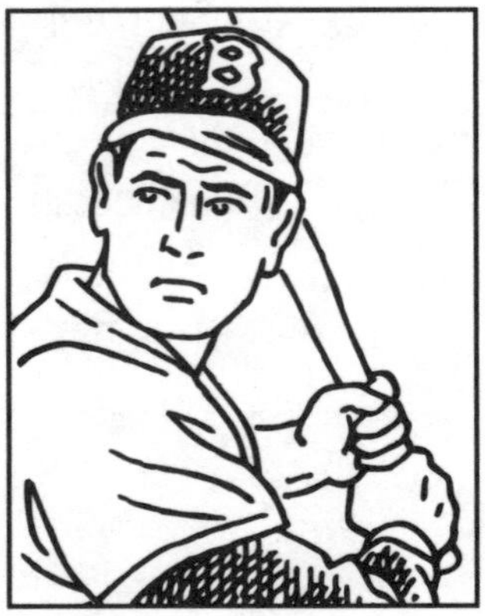

13. In what ways are cheetahs a perfect fit for life on grasslands? *Give at least one reason from each of the four sources provided.*

____

____

____

____

____

____

____

____

____

The Early Shift

Read each source below. Then complete the activities on pages 29–31.

Source 1

Mom knows that I'm always up at the crack of dawn on the weekends. That must be why she asked me to steer clear of Seth this Saturday morning.

"He's been hired to work the early shift at Hardy's Hardware," she explained. "Having a job will be a big change for him, so please be sensitive and respectful. He'll need time to get adjusted to his new routine."

I couldn't believe what I was hearing. "The *early* shift?" Seth is my older brother, so I know for a fact that he's the laziest person on the planet. Maybe there's somebody lazier on Mars, but Seth is the reigning champion on Earth.

Can my brother really drag himself out of bed before noon? To say that I am skeptical would be an understatement. But if Seth does succeed in getting out the door on time, I will be the first to congratulate him. It's a big change for him, and it won't be easy. In a weird way, I may even be proud of him.

Source 2

Hardy's Hardware

"Helping Make Your House a Home Since 1972"

Business Hours

	A.M. P.M.
Sunday	7:00–5:00
Monday	9:00–5:00
Tuesday	9:00–6:00
Wednesday	9:00–6:00
Thursday	9:00–6:00
Friday	9:00–7:00
Saturday	7:00–7:00

Source 3

As usual, I'm worried. I'm worried that Seth won't get up on Saturday and make it to work on time. Bob Hardy is not the most patient employer, and I can just imagine him sending Seth home before he even puts in an hour of work. Mr. Hardy wants Seth to arrive at the hardware store an hour before it opens for business. I've done the math in my head a million times, and I hope Seth has done it, too. It'll take him about 45 minutes to eat, shower, and get dressed. It will take him about 15 minutes to drive to the store.

I'm also worried that Seth *will* get up in time, but the new schedule will make him sick. It's hard getting up that early. Your body needs to adjust to getting less sleep. Seth will probably be grumpy and miserable, and he'll be in no mood to listen to Sammy. I'm sure Sammy will be up early on Saturday—like he is every Saturday—and he'll taunt Seth. I'm worried Seth is going to snap and yell at his little brother.

Tom keeps telling me not to worry so much. He says that I need to give our sons more credit. He says that this experience will help Seth learn to be more responsible and Sammy learn to be more sensitive. I hope that Tom is right, but I'm worried that he's not.

Source 4

It's like suddenly having a bucket of ice-cold water dumped on your head. One moment, I'm in the middle of a peaceful dream, and then my alarm is blaring and I'm waking into a nightmare. The clock says "4:44", which obviously is too early for the human brain to function properly. I desperately want to hit the snooze button, but I know that I can't do that. Today is my first day on the job on Hardy's Hardware. I want to show everyone—Mom, Dad, Mr. Hardy, even my little bother of a brother—that I can do this. I'm 17 years old, so I think it's time for me to grow up a bit. Plus, if I ever want to drive a decent car, I'm going to need to start earning money ASAP. I've got a lot riding on this job.

The Early Shift (cont.)

Name: _____

Part 1: Read each idea. Which source gives you this information? Fill in the correct bubble for each source. (Note: More than one bubble may be filled in for each idea.)

Information	Sources ➡	1	2	3	4
1. Seth is 17 years old.		○	○	○	○
2. Seth got a job at Hardy's Hardware.		○	○	○	○
3. Seth starts his job on Saturday.		○	○	○	○
4. Seth's brother is named Sammy.		○	○	○	○

Part 2: Fill in the bubble next to the best answer to each question.

5. Which of these times would most likely be described as "the crack of dawn"?

Ⓐ 12:15 a.m.   Ⓒ 8:50 a.m.

Ⓑ 4:25 a.m.   Ⓓ 5:30 p.m.

6. Which character's first name is not mentioned in any of the sources?

Ⓐ Seth's mom   Ⓒ Seth's brother

Ⓑ Seth's dad   Ⓓ Seth's employer

7. Which of these words from Source 1 means "having doubts"?

Ⓐ reigning   Ⓒ skeptical

Ⓑ sensitive   Ⓓ adjusted

8. Each answer choice below matches a character with a description. Which characterization is not correct?

Ⓐ Seth's mom, worries a lot

Ⓑ Seth, wants to be responsible

Ⓒ Sammy, makes jokes about his brother

Ⓓ Seth's dad, not known for being patient

Part 3: Search "The Early Shift" to find one example of each of the following. Then write the number of the source in which you located this information.

9. an abbreviation _____   Source #: _____

10. a hyphenated word _____   Source #: _____

The Early Shift *(cont.)*

Name: _____

Part 4: Refer back to the sources, and use complete sentences to answer these questions.

11. *Hyperbole* means "extreme exaggeration." A hyperbole is such an exaggeration that it cannot literally be true. There is at least one example of hyperbole in Sources 1, 3, and 4. Fill in the chart below. For each row, name the narrator and provide a quote that shows that narrator using hyperbole.

Source #	Narrator	Example of Hyperbole
1		
3		
4		

12. By getting up at 4:44, did Seth give himself enough time to get to work when Mr. Hardy wanted him to? Explain the math you used to get your answer.

_____

_____

_____

_____

_____

13. Write about Seth's first day from the point of view of the store owner, Mr. Hardy. Write about Mr. Hardy's thoughts in the morning before Seth arrived at work. Write about his thoughts when Seth arrived for work on time.

_____

_____

_____

_____

_____

_____

_____

_____

_____

The Golden Door

Read each source below. Then complete the activities on pages 33–35.

Source 1

It had been a long, trying journey from our old home in Italy to our new home in the United States. Conditions on our ship were abysmal. Our living quarters were cramped, and the "food" was awful. The year was 1899, and my father and I were immigrants on a ship bound for New York. Our plan was to find work in this new land and then send for Mama and my sisters.

Our destination was Ellis Island, where we would be inspected and hopefully allowed to pass through. To get there, our ship traveled northward up the Lower Bay of New York Harbor. We passed through the Narrows, which is a channel of water that leads to the Upper Bay. Soon we glimpsed the towering Statue of Liberty holding her torch up high on Liberty Island. She was the most majestic thing I had ever seen. As we sailed past her, I gazed in wonder. It was as if she was welcoming us to a bright new future. We passed so close to her, I could see every beautiful detail. Tears of relief streamed down my face.

To the northeast was the borough known as Manhattan. That was where we would look for work. But first we needed to stop on the small spot of land just north of Liberty Island. It was called Ellis Island. It would be there that Papa and I would take our first steps onto American soil. If we could make it through Ellis Island, we would enter into a land of opportunity.

Source 2

"The New Colossus" is a sonnet by Emma Lazarus. This poem was written in 1883 to help raise money to build a base on which the Statue of Liberty would sit. The Statue and its base were placed on Liberty Island in 1886. It wasn't until 1903, however, that Lazarus's poem was inscribed on the base.

Here is an excerpt from "The New Colossus":

. . . *cries she*

With silent lips. "Give me your tired, your poor,

Your huddled masses yearning to breathe free,

The wretched refuse of your teeming shore.

Send these, the homeless, tempest-tost to me,

I lift my lamp beside the golden door!"

Source 3

Glossary of Terms

borough (noun) – a part of a city (such as New York City)

colossus (noun) – a person or thing of great size, importance, or ability

immigrant (noun) – a person who comes to live permanently in a foreign country

sonnet (noun) – a poetic form that contains 14 lines

symbol (noun) – a thing that represents or stands for something else

Name: _____

Part 1: Read each idea. Which source gives you this information? Fill in the correct bubble for each source. (Note: More than one bubble may be filled in for each idea.)

Information	Sources ➡	1	2	3
1. A borough is a part of a city.		○	○	○
2. A sonnet is a type of poem.		○	○	○
3. The Statue of Liberty sits on an island.		○	○	○
4. Ellis Island is in New York Harbor.		○	○	○

Part 2: Fill in the bubble next to the best answer to each question.

5. What is the meaning of the word *trying* as it is used in the first sentence of Source 1?

Ⓐ attempting Ⓑ worrying Ⓒ eventful Ⓓ difficult

6. Choose the words that best complete this sentence about written material: _____ is a part from a larger whole.

Ⓐ An island Ⓒ An excerpt

Ⓑ A borough Ⓓ An immigrant

7. In order, what are the answers to these three questions from Source 2: Who cries with "silent lips"? Who are the "huddled masses"? What is the "golden door"?

Ⓐ Emma Lazarus, immigrants, New Jersey Ⓒ Statue of Liberty, America, immigrants

Ⓑ Statue of Liberty, immigrants, Ellis Island Ⓓ Emma Lazarus, America, New York

8. Could the narrator in Source 1 have been inspired by "The New Colossus" as his ship passed by Liberty Island?

Ⓐ No, because the poem had not yet been written.

Ⓑ No, because the poem was not yet inscribed on the Statue's base.

Ⓒ No, because the narrator did not like poetry.

Ⓓ Yes, because the poem symbolized a better life in a new country.

Part 3: Search "The Golden Door" to find one example of each of the following. Then write the number of the source in which you located this information.

9. a date from the 19th century _____ Source #: _____

10. an antonym of "temporarily" _____ Source #: _____

Name: _____

Part 4: Refer back to the sources, and use complete sentences to answer these questions.

11. The narrator in Source 1 says, "Conditions on our ship were abysmal." The word *abysmal* means "excessively bad." It is a much stronger, more descriptive, and more specific way to say "bad."

Rewrite the sentences below. As you do, replace all of the underlined words with much stronger words. Through the use of a few strong words, you can really paint a more vivid picture for your reader.

> My family <u>went</u> to the Statue of Liberty today.
> What a <u>big</u> monument! It was <u>very</u> <u>nice</u>.

_____

_____

_____

_____

12. From 1892–1954, over 12 million immigrants passed through Ellis Island on their way to becoming Americans. For these people, how might the Statue of Liberty have been a symbol who lifted her "lamp beside the golden door"? Use the geography of the area and the idea of what the Statue symbolized to answer the question.

_____

_____

_____

_____

_____

_____

_____

_____

_____

_____

The Golden Door (cont.)

Name: _____

13. Look at the map of New York Harbor below. Use the information from Source 1 to trace the narrator's journey. Label each stop on the map. Use these labels:

Ellis Island	Liberty Island	Lower Bay	Manhattan	The Narrows	Upper Bay

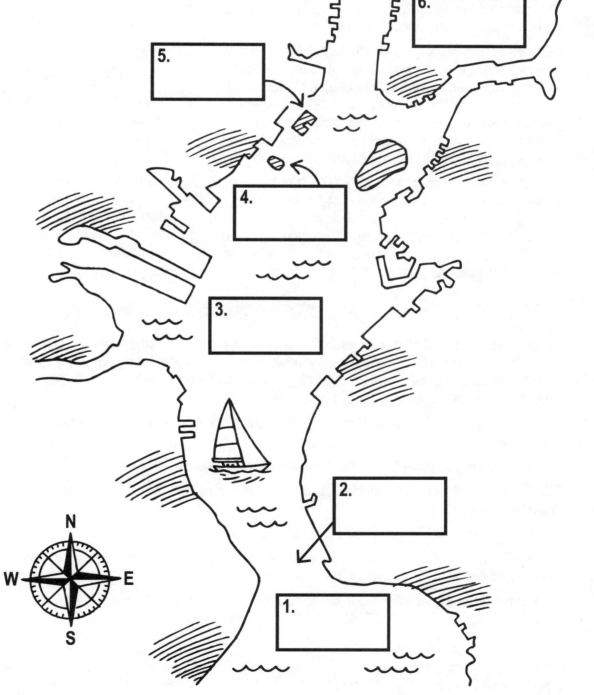

The Impossible Dream

Read each source below and on page 37. Then complete the activities on pages 38–40.

Source 1

**On This Day
in Baseball History**

April 15, 1997

Major League Baseball officially **retired uniform** #42 in honor of Jackie Robinson. This date marked the 50th anniversary of the day Robinson became the first African American in modern times to play in the major leagues. Throughout a 10-year career spent entirely with the Brooklyn Dodgers, Robinson faced many obstacles and battled widespread ignorance. However, his athletic excellence and professional demeanor on the field won him many fans and awards.

Since every team retired #42 on this date, that meant that no *new* players were allowed to wear it as their permanent number. However, a **grandfather clause** allowed players who were wearing the number prior to 1997 to continue wearing it until they retired from baseball. As a result, #42 was still worn on a regular basis by several players after 1997. By 2004, all but one of those players had retired.

Also, in games played on April 15, 2007, Major League Baseball allowed all players to wear #42 if they wished. Over 200 players took part in this tribute to Jackie Robinson. It has since become a tradition; and if you see a game on April 15 of any year, you may notice that all of the players are wearing the same number: 42.

What's It Mean?

to retire a uniform — to take a uniform number out of circulation and not allow it be worn again by another player

grandfather clause — an exemption for certain people whose previous rights or privileges would be affected by the requirements of a new rule

Source 2

My grandson lives and breathes baseball. Mikey knows all the current players. He knows most of the old ones, too. His favorite player is Derek Jeter, so naturally, Mikey wants to play shortstop for the Yankees when he grows up. I tell him that he can be anything he wants to be as long as he sets a goal and works hard for it. I believe that.

"I'm going to play for the Yankees one day," says Mikey. "I'm going to be a great hitter, and I'm going to wear a single-digit uniform number."

"I believe you will be great," I say. "But why do you need a single-digit uniform number?"

"All the great Yankees wore a single-digit number," Mikey informs me. "Lou Gehrig wore #4, Babe Ruth wore #3, and . . ."

"Derek Jeter wears #2," I say. "You should wear that uniform one day."

"No way!" says Mikey emphatically. "No one will ever wear #2 for the Yankees again. They won't let anyone else have Jeter's number when his career is over."

I just smile. I remember what it was like to be a kid and to love the Yankees. My favorite Yankee was Mickey Mantle. He wore #7. Maybe Mikey will get to wear that number one day.

Source 3

The New York Yankees are a team that is rich in tradition and success. As of 2014, they have won 27 championships, by far the most in Major League history. (The St. Louis Cardinals have won the second-most with 11.) Even the Yankees' uniforms can be said to be in a league of their own.

Due to their design, their uniforms are often referred to as the "Yankee pinstripes." This classic look ranks among the most recognizable and renowned jerseys in all of professional sports. Yankee uniforms are also unique for a variety of reasons:

⚲ In 1929, the Yankees became the first team to put numbers on their uniforms.

⚲ As of 2014, the Yankees are the only team that doesn't put its players' names on the backs of any of their jerseys.

⚲ As of 2014, the Yankees have retired more uniform numbers (17) than any other team. (That number is expected to rise to 18 when Derek Jeter's #2 is retired soon after the 2014 season.) The following players and managers have had their Yankee uniform numbers retired:

Number	Player(s)	Position(s)	Date Retired
1	Billy Martin	2B, M	8/10/1986
3	Babe Ruth	RF	6/13/1948
4	Lou Gehrig	1B	7/4/1939
5	Joe DiMaggio	CF	4/18/1952
6	Joe Torre	M	8/23/2014
7	Mickey Mantle	CF	6/8/1969
8	Bill Dickey	C	7/22/1972
8	Yogi Berra	C	7/22/1972
9	Roger Maris	RF	7/21/1984
10	Phil Rizzuto	SS	8/4/1985
15	Thurman Munson	C	8/3/1979
16	Whitey Ford	SP	8/3/1974
23	Don Mattingly	1B	8/31/1997
32	Elson Howard	C	7/21/1984
37	Casey Stengel	M	8/8/1970
42	Mariano Rivera	RP	9/22/2013
44	Reggie Jackson	RF	8/14/1993
49	Ron Guidry	SP	8/23/2003

Position Key: C (catcher), 1B (first baseman), 2B (second baseman), SS (shortstop), 3B (third baseman), LF (left fielder), CF (center fielder), RF (right fielder), SP (starting pitcher), RP (relief pitcher), M (manager)

The Impossible Dream (cont.)

Name: _____

Part 1: Read each idea. Which source gives you this information? Fill in the correct bubble for each source. (Note: More than one bubble may be filled in for each idea.)

Information	Sources ➡	1	2	3
1. The New York Yankees have retired the #7 uniform.		○	○	○
2. The New York Yankees have retired the #42 uniform.		○	○	○
3. Mickey Mantle wore #7 for the New York Yankees.		○	○	○
4. Derek Jeter wore #2 for the New York Yankees.		○	○	○

Part 2: Fill in the bubble next to the best answer to each question.

5. On which of these occasions did Major League Baseball first allow all players to wear Jackie Robinson's #42 during games?

   Ⓐ the 50th anniversary of Robinson's birthday   Ⓒ the 60th anniversary of Robinson's first game

   Ⓑ the 50th anniversary of Robinson's first game   Ⓓ the 60th anniversary of Robinson's birthday

6. In Source 2, which of the following facts is *implied* but not directly stated in the text?

   Ⓐ Derek Jeter is Mikey's favorite baseball player.   Ⓒ Derek Jeter plays the shortstop position.

   Ⓑ Derek Jeter wears uniform #2.   Ⓓ Derek Jeter plays for the New York Yankees.

7. No Yankees who regularly played these positions have had their numbers retired.

   Ⓐ 3B and LF   Ⓒ SP and LF

   Ⓑ 3B and RF   Ⓓ LF and RP

8. This unit is titled "The Impossible Dream" because Mikey

   Ⓐ will never be allowed to play for the New York Yankees.

   Ⓑ will never be allowed to wear a single-digit number for the Yankees.

   Ⓒ will never have his number retired by Major League Baseball.

   Ⓓ will never be allowed to wear #42 for any team during any game.

Part 3: Search "The Impossible Dream" to find one example of each of the following. Then write the number of the source in which you located this information.

   9. an adjective meaning "easily identified" _____ Source #: _____

   10. an adverb meaning "in a forceful way" _____ Source #: _____

The Impossible Dream *(cont.)*

Name: _____

Part 4: Refer back to the sources to answer these questions.

11. Two sets of Yankees had their numbers retired on the same date (month and day) but in different years. Complete the diagrams below by naming those two sets of Yankees.

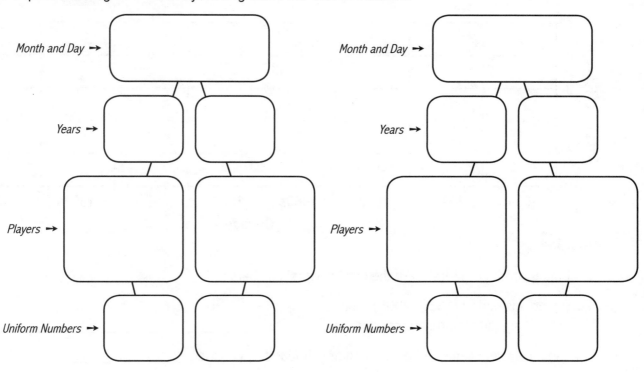

12. Mariano Rivera played his entire career with the New York Yankees and retired from baseball in 2013. Using that knowledge, along with the facts from the sources, prove or disprove the statement in the box below. Use complete sentences.

> **Statement**
>
> Mariano Rivera began wearing #42 before April 1997, and he was the last baseball player allowed to wear #42 on a regular basis.

_____

_____

_____

_____

_____

_____

The Impossible Dream *(cont.)*

Name: _____

Part 4 *(cont.)*:

13. Create a bar graph below to show how many Yankee players had their numbers retired in each decade from the 1930s to the 2000s (2000–2009). Then follow the directions given below the graph.

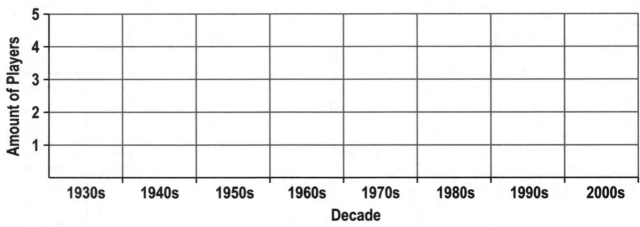

Directions:

A. During which decade(s) were the most players' numbers retired? _____

B. During this period (1930–2009), what is the average amount retired per decade? _____

Use a complete sentence to explain how you found this answer. _____

_____

C. What percentage of players' numbers retired between 1930–2009 were retired during the 1980s? _____

Use a complete sentence to explain how you found this answer. _____

_____

D. Write your own unique question based on the graph. Include four answer choices, only one of which could be correct.

Question: _____

Answer Choices:

a. _____

b. _____

c. _____

d. _____

Selling Snacks

Read each source below and on page 42. Then complete the activities on pages 43–45.

Source 1

HEALTH NUTZ
Introduces
5 new varieties of
Superfood Snacks

Blueberry Blasts $4.09

Carob Swirls $2.99

Chia Squares $4.29

Kale Crunchies $3.59

Walnutty Wafers $2.29

(price per 12-ounce package)

Source 2

Glossary of Business Terms

consumer — a person who purchases goods and services for personal use

profit — a financial gain; the difference between the amount earned and the amount spent in producing something

quarter — a period of three months used in reference to a company's expenses and earnings; there are four quarters per year

---

Source 3

Attention Team Health Nutz:

Our sales figures are in for the new line of Superfood Snacks.

➤ **Chart A** below shows the number of packages of each snack product that were purchased by consumers in the 1st quarter of this year.

➤ **Chart B** shows the cost for producing one package of each snack.

Chart A: Estimated Sales for 1st Quarter of 2016 (January–March)

Product	Packages Sold
Blueberry Blasts	1,200
Carob Swirls	960
Chia Squares	750
Kale Crunchies	900
Walnutty Wafers	1,000

Chart B: Cost of Production

Product	Cost Per Package
Blueberry Blasts	$2.84
Carob Swirls	$1.49
Chia Squares	$2.29
Kale Crunchies	$1.79
Walnutty Wafers	$0.89

We need to use the information given in these charts to determine our profits for the previous quarter and to estimate our sales for the upcoming quarter. I want this information by no later than the end of the business day tomorrow.

And, as always, thank you for your great effort!

Keith Knutzen
Owner

Health Nutz, Inc.

Name: _____

Part 1: Read each idea. Which source gives you this information? Fill in the correct bubble for each source. (Note: More than one bubble may be filled in for each idea.)

Information	Sources ➡	1	2	3
1. Health Nutz sells a product called Chia Squares.		○	○	○
2. It costs $2.29 to produce a package of Chia Squares.		○	○	○
3. Consumers pay $4.29 for a package of Chia Squares.		○	○	○
4. Consumers are people who buy products.		○	○	○

Part 2: Fill in the bubble next to the best answer to each question.

5. Based on the sales figures, which product was the least popular with consumers?

Ⓐ Carob Swirls   Ⓒ Kale Crunchies

Ⓑ Chia Squares   Ⓓ Walnutty Wafers

6. Which of these purchases would cost the consumer the least amount of money?

Ⓐ three boxes of Walnutty Wafers

Ⓑ two boxes of Blueberry Blasts

Ⓒ one box of Carob Swirls and one box of Chia Squares

Ⓓ two boxes of Kale Crunchies

7. What is the cost per ounce of Walnutty Wafers?

Ⓐ $2.29   Ⓒ less than $0.20

Ⓑ just over $0.20   Ⓓ none of the above

8. If the sales figures in Source 3 hold true for the next three quarters, how many packages of Blueberry Blasts will the company sell in one year?

Ⓐ 600   Ⓒ 2,400

Ⓑ 1,200   Ⓓ 4,800

Part 3: Search "Selling Snacks" to find one example of each of the following. Then write the number of the source in which you located this information.

9. a synonym for "guess" _____   Source #: _____

10. a synonym for "approaching" _____   Source #: _____

Selling Snacks *(cont.)*

Name: _____

Part 4: Complete questions 11–13 to determine Health Nutz's profits for the sale of Superfood Snacks.

11. What equation would you use to determine the profit for each package of snack sold?

- Fill in the blank box with words that complete the equation.

- For A–E, use the equation to determine the profit for each type of snack. Use Sources 1 and 3 to find the data to complete each equation.

Equation: amount consumers pay per package

$$- \boxed{}$$

profit per package

A. Blueberry Blasts: ___$4.09___ – _____ = ___$1.25___

B. Carob Swirls: _____ – _____ = _____

C. Chia Squares: _____ – _____ = _____

D. Kale Crunchies: _____ – _____ = _____

E. Walnutty Wafers: _____ – _____ = _____

12. Now determine the total profit per snack.

- For the equation, fill in the blank box with the correct operational sign (**+**, **–**, **×**, or **÷**).

- For A–E, use the equation to determine the profit for each type of snack. Use Source 3, along with your answers from question #11, to find the data to complete each equation.

Equation: profit per package

$$\boxed{} \text{ packages sold}$$

total profit per snack

A. Blueberry Blasts: ___$1.25___ $\boxed{}$ ___1,200___ = _____

B. Carob Swirls: _____ $\boxed{}$ _____ = _____

C. Chia Squares: _____ $\boxed{}$ _____ = _____

D. Kale Crunchies: _____ $\boxed{}$ _____ = _____

E. Walnutty Wafers: _____ $\boxed{}$ _____ = _____

Name: _____

Part 4 *(cont.):*

13. Use your results from #12 to answer the following questions.

A. Which snack yielded the highest profit in the first quarter of 2016?

_____

B. Which snack yielded the lowest profit in the first quarter of 2016?

_____

C. Which two snacks had the same profit in the first quarter of 2016?

_____

_____

D. The following two graphs each show the data from #12. One is a pie chart, and the other is a bar graph.

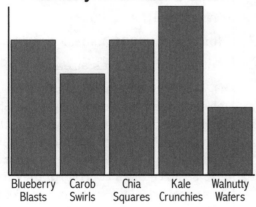

**Profit Earnings Per Snack
January 2016–March 2016**

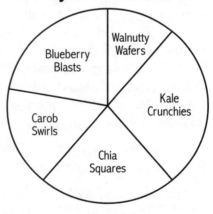

**Profit Earnings Per Snack
January 2016–March 2016**

Which graph best illustrates the data? Explain your answer.

_____

_____

_____

_____

_____

_____

In More Than One Place

Read each source below. Then complete the activities on pages 47—49.

Source 1

Matt said, "I'm confused. Our group is visiting two major cities next week. We're going to London and Dublin. So we'll be in the United Kingdom, right? Or will we be in Great Britain? How about the British Isles? I keep hearing all of these different terms, and I don't know what each one means."

"It's simple," Kim said. "While you are in London, you will be in Great Britain and also in the United Kingdom. You see, London is the capital of England, and England is the largest country on the island of Great Britain. Great Britain is mostly made up of three countries: England, Scotland, and Wales. Scotland is to the north of England, while Wales is to the west. Got it?"

Matt muttered, "Umm, I think so."

Kim continued, "Now the United Kingdom includes Great Britain and the country of Northern Ireland. It does not include the Republic of Ireland, the capital of which is Dublin. Northern Ireland is to the north of the Republic of Ireland. Together, these two places make up the island of Ireland."

"Wait!" blurted Matt. "So what about the British Isles? What are those?"

"The British Isles," said Kim, "is all of it! It's Great Britain *and* Ireland, along with about 6,000 other small islands."

Looking dazed, Matt said, "I think I'm going to have to draw up a chart or something to keep this all straight."

Source 2

Prime Meridian

This line of longitude extends from north to south and divides Earth into two equal halves, or hemispheres. Places to the west of the Prime Meridian are considered to be in the Western Hemisphere, while those to the east are in the Eastern Hemisphere.

Note: The Prime Meridian is an imaginary line, and some disagree on where it is. In 1884, the location of the Prime Meridian was agreed on at the International Meridian Conference, which was held in Washington, D.C. This agreed-upon line of longitude is the one that passes through Greenwich in the city of London, England.

Source 3

From: matthewq1993@email.com

To: kimmyq1991@email.com

Subject: two places at once!

Hi Kim! London is fabulous. I've already seen the London Eye, the Shard, and the Monument. The neatest thing, though, might have been the Royal Observatory in Greenwich, London. In the observatory's courtyard, they have a strip of stainless steel that marks the Prime Meridian. I'll send you a picture someone took of me standing with one foot on either side of this strip. That means I had one foot in the Western Hemisphere and one foot in the Eastern Hemisphere!

Tell the whole family back home in Boston that I love them. Even though I'm thousands of miles away, I'm always with them in my thoughts.

Love, Matt

In More Than One Place (cont.)

Name: _____

Part 1: Read each idea. Which source gives you this information? Fill in the correct bubble for each source. (Note: More than one bubble may be filled in for each idea.)

Information Sources ➡	1	2	3
1. The Prime Meridian is an imaginary line of longitude.	○	○	○
2. The Prime Meridian passes through Greenwich, London.	○	○	○
3. The Royal Observatory is located in London.	○	○	○
4. London is located in Great Britain.	○	○	○

Part 2: Fill in the bubble next to the best answer to each question.

5. Which of the cities mentioned in the sources is not the capital of its country?

Ⓐ Boston

Ⓑ Dublin

Ⓒ London

Ⓓ Washington, D.C.

6. Matt's email address was created by using his first name, his last initial, and the year he was born. Using that information, how many years before he was born did the International Meridian Conference take place?

Ⓐ 99

Ⓑ 101

Ⓒ 107

Ⓓ 109

7. Which term best describes the function of the underlined word in the following phrase: "In the observatory's courtyard."

Ⓐ proper noun

Ⓑ proper adjective

Ⓒ possessive noun

Ⓓ action verb

8. Using the information given in the 2nd paragraph of Source 1, which of the following can you infer about Great Britain?

Ⓐ It is located entirely in the Western Hemisphere.

Ⓑ It is located entirely in the Eastern Hemisphere.

Ⓒ It is completely surrounded by water.

Ⓓ It is the capital of the British Isles.

Part 3: Search "In More Than One Place" to find one example of each of the following. Then write the number of the source in which you located this information.

9. an adjective meaning "occurring between many nations" _____ Source #: _____

10. a verb meaning "said suddenly and without consideration" _____ Source #: _____

In More Than One Place *(cont.)*

Name: _____

Part 4: Refer back to the sources, and use complete sentences to answer these questions.

11. On the map below, label the following places:

> **England   Northern Ireland   The Republic of Ireland   Scotland   Wales**

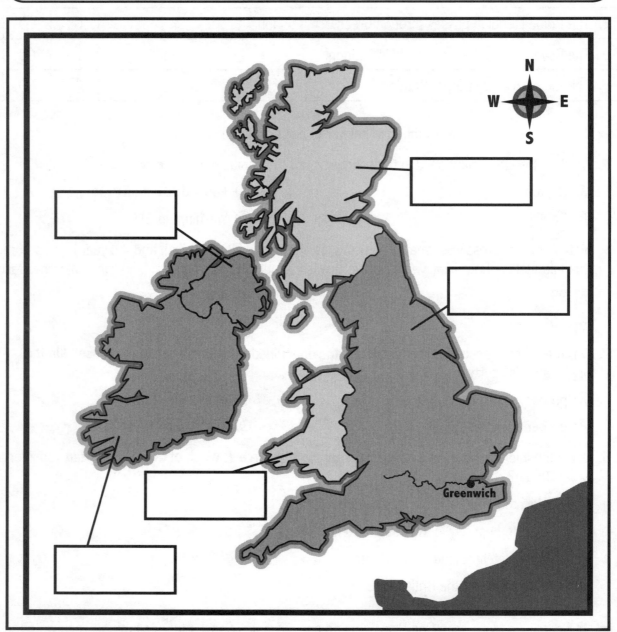

Draw a straight, dotted line to represent the Prime Meridian. Use the information given in the sources to determine exactly where it should be located. Then fill in the blank to complete this statement:

Ireland is located entirely within the _____ Hemisphere.

In More Than One Place (cont.)

Name: _____

Part 4 *(cont.)*:

12. Make a chart to help Matt. Write in the following place names in the correct columns to show where each one is located. Note: Some places may belong in more than one column.

Dublin	Greenwich	Northern Ireland	Scotland
England	London	The Republic of Ireland	Wales

The British Isles	Great Britain	Ireland	United Kingdom

13. This unit is titled "In More Than One Place." Why is this title appropriate? Describe all the ways in which the title fits this collection of sources.

_____

_____

_____

_____

_____

_____

_____

_____

_____

_____

More Rare Than Gold

Read each source below and on page 51. Then complete the activities on pages 52–53.

Source 1

MONTI GETS HIS GOLD

February 1968

At long last, one of the world's greatest sportsman, Italian bobsled pilot Eugenio Monti, has won Olympic gold. In the recently concluded 1968 Winter Olympic Games, Monti earned gold medals for both the two-man and four-man bobsled events.

The 40-year-old Monti has now competed in three Winter Olympic Games. It was during the 1964 Games, however, that he became famous for more than just his physical achievements. At those Winter Olympic Games, Monti twice helped his fellow competitors when they were in need. First, he aided the two-man British team by lending them a bolt when one of theirs had broken. Without his support, the British team would not have been able to compete. With his assistance, they won the gold medal. Then, Monti helped repair a damaged axle on the Canadian four-man team's sled. Once again, this allowed his opponents to win the gold. For these acts of generosity, Monti was awarded the Pierre de Coubertin award for sportsmanship. He was the first person to receive this prestigious award.

Monti's Medals		
Year	Event	Medal
1956	two-man bobsled	silver
1956	four-man bobsled	silver
1964	two-man bobsled	bronze
1964	four-man bobsled	bronze
1968	two-man bobsled	gold
1968	four-man bobsled	gold

* Due to economic factors, the bobsled event was not a part of the 1960 Winter Olympic Games.

Source 2

The Pierre de Coubertin Medal

- also known as The True Spirit of Sportsmanship medal
- named for Pierre de Coubertin, who created the International Olympic Committee (IOC) in 1894
- given by the IOC to athletes who have shown exemplary sportsmanship while competing in Olympic events
- first recipient was Eugenio Monti (in 1964)
- awarded to four athletes during the 20th century
  Eugenio Monti (Italy, 1964)
  Luz Long (Germany, 1964)
  Karl Heinz Klee (Austria, 1977)
  Lawrence Lemieux (Canada, 1988)

Source 3

Jesse Owens (1913–1980) was a star athlete, but on this day he sat dejected. His Olympic dreams hung in the balance. A long jump of 7.15 meters was all he needed to advance to the next round. Owens was the man who owned the world record in this event for his jump of 8.13 meters the previous year. And on this day, he had easily cleared the required distance on his first two jumps, but neither one counted. On both attempts, the American athlete had stepped across the foul line prior to jumping. If he did this once more, he would be disqualified.

It was at that point that one of his opponents, Luz Long (1913–1943) of Germany, came over to encourage Owens and give him a piece of advice. Long suggested that since Owens' jumps were always well in excess of 7.15 meters, he should take off from a spot a few inches in front of the foul line.

Owens tried this approach, and he was successful. This led to a finals showdown between Owens and Long. The result? Owens won the gold medal with a leap of 8.06 meters, while Long took home the silver for second place for jumping 7.87 meters. Each distance broke the previous record for the Olympic long jump (or "broad jump" as it was known at the time).

Olympic athlete Luz Long

An act of sportsmanship such as this is noteworthy on its own. What made Long's gesture truly historic was the context in which it took place. These events unfolded during the 1936 Summer Olympic Games, which were held in Berlin, Germany. 1936 was three years **after** Adolf Hitler and the Nazi Party had become the ruling party in Germany and three years **before** their attacks on people, races, and countries began World War II. One of the Nazi Party's main beliefs was that people who came from a specific northern European race were superior to people from other races. As an African American, Jesse Owens belonged to one of the races the Nazi Party deemed inferior.

Not only did Long advise Owens, he also befriended him. He was the first one to congratulate Owens after his record-breaking jump, and the two competitors walked off the field arm-in-arm. To show such compassion toward Owens would likely be seen as an act of defiance to his country's leaders. About Long, Owens later said, "It took a lot of courage for him to befriend me in front of Hitler."

The 1936 Games were the only ones in which Long competed. He later became a member of the German army and fought in World War II. He was killed by Allied Forces* during combat. In 1964 he was posthumously awarded the Pierre de Coubertin Medal for demonstrating the true spirit of sportsmanship. He was the second person to ever receive this high honor.

In World War II, the Allied Forces mainly consisted of the militaries from Britain, China, France, the Soviet Union, and the United States.

Name: _____

Part 1: Read each idea. Which source gives you this information? Fill in the correct bubble for each source. (Note: More than one bubble may be filled in for each idea.)

Information	Sources ➡	1	2	3
1. Eugenio Monti received two Olympic gold medals.		○	○	○
2. Eugenio Monti received the Pierre de Coubertin medal.		○	○	○
3. The Pierre de Coubertin medal was first given in the 1960s.		○	○	○
4. Luz Long from Germany was also awarded the Pierre de Coubertin.		○	○	○

Part 2: Fill in the bubble(s) next to the best answer(s) to each question.

5. How much longer was Owens' world-record-setting long jump than his Olympic-record-setting long jump?

Ⓐ 0.7 meters

Ⓑ 0.07 meters

Ⓒ 0.19 meters

Ⓓ 0.98 meters

6. Which of the following events did not take place during the 1960s?

Ⓐ Eugenio Monti was the given the Pierre de Coubertin award.

Ⓑ Eugenio Monti won his first Olympic gold medals.

Ⓒ Eugenio Monti won his first Olympic medals.

Ⓓ Eugenio Monti turned 30 years old.

7. Which of the sources contains a sidebar?

Ⓐ Source 1

Ⓑ Source 2

Ⓒ Source 3

Ⓓ all of the above

8. Reread the final paragraph of Source 3. You can infer from the information given that the word *posthumously* means _____.

Ⓐ "after the Olympic Games"

Ⓑ "after death"

Ⓒ "during combat"

Ⓓ "during World War II"

Part 3: Search "More Rare Than Gold" to find **two-word phrases** with the following meanings. Then write the number of the source in which you located this information.

9. "just ended" _____ Source #: _____

10. "considered to be worth less" _____ Source #: _____

More Rare Than Gold *(cont.)*

Name: _____

Part 4: Refer back to the sources, and use complete sentences to answer these questions.

11. Fill in the timeline below with important events from Olympic history. Add one date and event in each section provided. The first one is done for you.

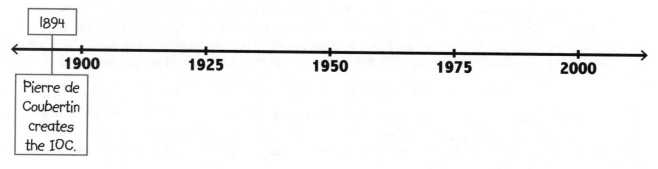

12. Word choice is a key ingredient to good writing. Reread the final paragraph of Source 1. In this passage, the writer tries to avoid overusing forms of the word *help*. Which words does the writer use in this word's place? As a reader, how do you feel this paragraph would change if the writer repeated the word *help* of choosing replacements for it?

_____

_____

_____

_____

13. Compare and contrast Monti and Long, the first two athletes to receive the Pierre de Coubertin award. Mention the similarities and differences in their stories.

_____

_____

_____

_____

_____

_____

_____

_____

Around a Long Time

Read each source below and on page 55. Then complete the activities on pages 56–57.

Source 1

"What is that you're drawing over and over again?" asked Isa. She was craning her neck to look at the odd marks Mark was making on his paper.

"I'm practicing my calligraphy," said Mark. Seeing that Isa didn't understand what he meant, Mark continued, "Calligraphy is a form of writing used in China, Japan, and Korea. It has been used in China for thousands of years! To this day, those who do it well are highly respected. Master calligraphers combine the creativity of an artist with the technical skill of a craftsman. I am just learning."

"That's a lot of history. Does that symbol you're drawing mean something?"

"This is the *yong* character," said Mark. "*Yong* means 'permanence' or 'eternity.' This character is special because it is made up of the eight most basic strokes that calligraphers use. These strokes are called 'The Eight Principles of *Yong*.' It's very important to practice them over and over again. Do you want to try?"

Isa grabbed the calligraphy brush and tried to copy Mark's *yong* character. Mark stopped her and showed her that she needed to do the strokes in a particular order.

"First," he said, "you need to make a dot at the top. Then, your second stroke is called the 'Bridle.' It is a short, horizontal line that curves up just a little bit."

Isa's hand was unsteady, and her strokes did not look like Mark's. She giggled a bit and said, "I can see why this *yong* character means 'eternity.' It would take me a really *yong* time to learn how to do it correctly."

Mark chuckled and shook his head, "That was a silly joke, but you made me laugh."

Source 2

pun

A **pun** is a form of expression that takes advantage of similarities in sound and/or meaning between words and phrases. Puns are usually meant to be humorous.

Examples of early puns can be found in ancient texts written thousands of years ago.

Also Known As:

- ⊙ word play
- ⊙ a play on words
- ⊙ paronomasia (pair uh no ma zee uh)

Examples:

- ▶ Why did the turkey cross the road?
  - – to prove he wasn't chicken
- ▶ Why are fish so smart?
  - – because they live in schools

Around a Long Time *(cont.)*

The Eight Principles of *Yong*

The *yong* character looks like this:

It has the following meanings:

"Eternity"

"Forever"

"Permanence"

To write the *yong* character, one must use the eight principal strokes of calligraphy:

Number	Stroke	Names
1	永	"Sideway" — "Dot" — "Strange stone"
2	永	"Bridle" — "Horizontal" — "Jade table"
3	永	"Crossbow" — "Iron staff" — "Iron pillar"
4	永	"Jump" — "Hook" — "Pincer of a crab"
5	永	"Horsewhip" — "Raise" — "Tiger's tooth"
6	永	"Passing lightly" — "Bend, curve" — "Horn of rhinoceros"
7	永	"Short slant" — "Bird pecking"
8	永	"Passing forcefully" — "Golden knife"

Name: _____

Part 1: Read each idea. Which source gives you this information? Fill in the correct bubble for each source. (Note: More than one bubble may be filled in for each idea.)

Information	Sources ➡	1	2	3
1. Calligraphy has been around for thousands of years.		○	○	○
2. The calligraphic character *yong* means "eternity."		○	○	○
3. The first stroke needed to make *yong* is a dot.		○	○	○
4. The second stroke needed to make *yong* is "Bridle."		○	○	○

Part 2: Fill in the bubble(s) next to the best answer(s) to each question.

5. Which of these sets of fractions and percentages show how many of the Eight Principles of *Yong* are named after animals?

   Ⓐ $\frac{1}{4}$, 25%　　　　Ⓑ $\frac{1}{2}$, 50%　　　　Ⓒ $\frac{3}{8}$, 37.5%　　　　Ⓓ $\frac{4}{8}$, 50%

6. Which of these statements are true about both puns and calligraphy?

   Ⓐ They are forms of expression.

   Ⓑ They have been around a long time.

   Ⓒ Mark practices using them.

   Ⓓ Isa practices using them.

7. Which of these calligraphic strokes makes a thick vertical line?

   Ⓐ "Hook"　　　　　　　　　　Ⓒ "Tiger's tooth"

   Ⓑ "Iron pillar"　　　　　　　　Ⓓ "Horn of rhinoceros"

8. In Source 3, which of these words are used as adjectives?

   Ⓐ principal　　　　　　　　　Ⓒ pincer

   Ⓑ Principles　　　　　　　　　Ⓓ Iron

Part 3: Search "Around a Long Time" to find one example of each of the following. Then write the number of the source in which you located this information.

  9. a noun with six syllables _____　Source #: _____

 10. a synonym for "funny" _____　Source #: _____

Name: _____

Part 4: Refer back to the sources, and use complete sentences to answer these questions.

11. Many jokes are divided into two parts: the setup and the punchline. Look at this setup to a joke:

Why did the spider turn on his computer?

Which of the following punchlines would be needed to make this joke a pun? Fill in the circle next to the correct answer choice below. Then explain why the completed joke is a pun.

Ⓐ to check his e-mail

Ⓑ to look at his website

Ⓒ to send out a few tweets

_____

_____

_____

_____

12. In Source 1, Isa makes a joke. Quote each part of the joke exactly, and then explain why the joke is a pun.

Setup: _____

Punchline: _____

Why It's a Pun: _____

_____

_____

_____

13. Choose one of the "Eight Principles of *Yong*." Fill out the lines below:

Stroke Name: _____

Stroke Number: _____

In your own words, describe how the stroke is made. In which direction does it go? Is it thick or thin? Does it change in any way from beginning to end?

_____

_____

_____

_____

Six Honest Serving-Men

Read each source below. Then complete the activities on pages 59–61.

Source 1

from "The Elephant's Child"
by Rudyard Kipling (1902)

I keep six honest serving-men
(They taught me all I knew);
Their names are What and Why and When
And How and Where and Who.

Source 2

Glossary of Newspaper Terms

article — a written piece about a topic

byline — the name of the reporter who wrote the article

5 Ws and an H — questions (Who, What, When, Where, Why, and How) an article should answer about the subject being reported

headline — title of the article, usually set in large, bold type

inverted triangle — a diagram shaped like an upside-down triangle that shows the content of an article, with the most important items listed at the top, and the least important items listed at the bottom

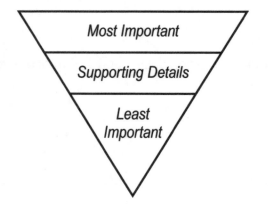

Most Important

Supporting Details

Least Important

Source 3

WILDCATS SUFFER FIRST LOSS
by Aurora Lee

After starting the season 9-0, Wilson High lost its first game on Thursday. Playing in front of their home crowd, the Hornets from Jefferson High improved to 7-3 as they defeated the Wildcats behind the pitching of Ty King. King struck out 12 Wildcats on his way to a 4-1 victory.

The Wildcats' top pitcher, Scott Shay, cruised through the first five innings. His teammates scored a run in the top of the first inning, and Shay held the Hornets scoreless into the bottom of the sixth. It was then that Shay suddenly had trouble throwing strikes. He walked three batters before allowing a bases-clearing double to Jefferson's Mark Clark. Clark later stole third base and came home on a wild pitch. Those were all the runs King needed, as he tossed a scoreless seventh inning to secure the victory.

"It's a big win for us," said Hornets' coach Art Moore. "To beat an undefeated team like Wilson High, you really need a great effort from everyone. We got some clutch hitting, and what can I say about Ty King? He showed why he's the ace of our pitching staff."

The Hornets travel to Cook High next week, while the Wildcats host the Kennedy Cougars on Tuesday.

Six Honest Serving-Men (cont.)

Name: _____

Part 1: Read each idea from Source 3. In which **paragraph** in Source 3 is this information located? Fill in the correct bubble. (Note: More than one bubble may be filled in for each idea.)

Information	Paragraphs ➡	1	2	3	4
1. Art Moore coaches the Hornets.		◯	◯	◯	◯
2. Ty King pitches for the Hornets.		◯	◯	◯	◯
3. Mark Clark scored on a wild pitch.		◯	◯	◯	◯
4. Wilson High was undefeated before this game.		◯	◯	◯	◯

Part 2: Fill in the bubble next to the best answer to each question.

5. Who is the author of "The Elephant's Child"?

   Ⓐ Art Moore   Ⓒ Aurora Lee

   Ⓑ Rudyard Kipling   Ⓓ Scott Slinger

6. Which school is most likely **not** named after a U.S. president?

   Ⓐ Wilson   Ⓒ Cook

   Ⓑ Jefferson   Ⓓ Kennedy

7. The coach describes Ty King as the "ace of our pitching staff." What does he mean?

   Ⓐ Ty is the star of the staff.

   Ⓑ Ty is the only pitcher on the staff.

   Ⓒ Ty is a new player on the team.

   Ⓓ Ty wins every game in which he pitches.

8. After the game against Jefferson High, what was the Wildcats' win-loss record for the season?

   Ⓐ 4-1   Ⓒ 7-3

   Ⓑ 9-1   Ⓓ 4-2

Part 3: Search "Six Honest Serving-Men" to find one example of each of the following. Then write the number of the source in which you located this information.

9. a headline _____ Source #: _____

10. a byline _____ Source #: _____

Name: _____

Part 4: Refer back to the sources, and use complete sentences to answer these questions.

11. Look at the scoreboards below. Which one accurately shows the scoreboard for the game between the Wildcats and the Hornets? Explain your answer. (Hint: The numbers to the right of each team's name show how many runs that team scored in each inning.)

Scoreboard 1

Inning

Team	1	2	3	4	5	6	7	Game
Wildcats	1	0	0	0	0	0	0	1
Hornets	0	0	0	0	0	4		4

Scoreboard 2

Inning

Team	1	2	3	4	5	6	7	Game
Wildcats	0	1	0	0	0	0	0	1
Hornets	0	0	0	0	4	0		4

_____

_____

_____

_____

_____

_____

12. What is another name for the "six honest serving-men" referred to in Source 1, and why are these six elements important to a newspaper article?

_____

_____

_____

_____

_____

_____

_____

_____

_____

_____

Six Honest Serving-Men (cont.)

Name: _____

Part 4 (cont.):

13. Look at the inverted triangle described in Source 2. Each section is labeled. Below are some facts given in the article from Source 3. Write a letter label (A, B, or C) to show the section of the triangle in which each part would belong. Then explain your answer. The first one has been done for you.

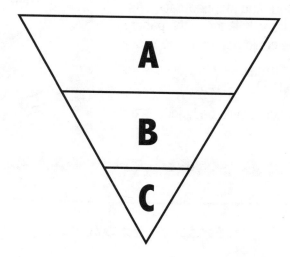

_____A_____ ❶ The Wildcats lost their first game of the season. __This information is very__

__important to the story, as it is even mentioned in the headline.__

_____ ❷ The Wildcats have a game against Kennedy next week. _____

_____

_____ ❸ Scott Shay pitched well against Wilson last week. _____

_____

_____ ❹ The Hornets beat the Wildcats 4-1. _____

_____

_____ ❺ Scott Shay walked three batters in the sixth inning. _____

_____

_____ ❻ Ty King was the winning pitcher for the Hornets. _____

_____

A Cache of Cash on Cache

Read each source below and on page 63. Then complete the activities on pages 64–65.

Source 1

With great excitement, Kyle ran 10 blocks to his friend Kayla's house. The piece of paper he gripped tightly in his right hand fluttered in the wind as he ran.

He knocked on her front door and stepped back. As soon as Kayla opened the door, Kyle thrust the paper in front of her face where she could get a good look at it.

Gasping for air, Kyle said, "Treasure. On Cache Ave. Four clues. Let's go. Now!"

"It makes sense that a treasure would be hidden in that location," said Kayla.

Source 2

cache

(pronounced *cash*)

a hidden supply of something

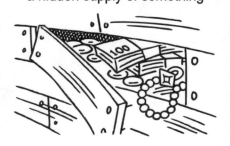

Source 3

Attention, Explorers!

If it is treasure you seek, then it is treasure you shall find. Just be the first to decipher my clues. A valuable treasure is hidden somewhere on my property at 312 Cache Ave. What treasure, you ask? A jar containing money! How much? Put the numbers four, five, six, and seven in alphabetical order; then put a decimal point to the left of the final number. That will tell you how much this treasure is worth. Where is this treasure hidden? Ahh, that is a mystery you must solve. Find a quartet of clues, and you will have your answer.

Begin your quest at the mailbox. Walk straight along the side of the house, toward the backyard. Beware the roses! They have thorns, and they hold no key to the treasure you seek. Don't stop until you reach the place where man's best friend sleeps each night. There you will find a letter. It is your first clue.

Next, walk across the backyard. Stay close to the house, where it is shady. You don't need to look at the device on the wall to know that it is a warm day. Instead you should *find the time* to collect clue number two.

From there, go around the corner and head north toward Cache Ave. Don't bother with the trash or the place where automobiles sleep at night. Keep moving until a large, natural object blocks your path to the street. Look up. The third clue is ripe and ready to be picked.

You're almost done! Turn around and march toward the backyard. Now you're really cooking! You need just one more clue. There it is, hanging from the outdoor grill. It's the final letter. Put your clues together. What do they spell? That is where you will find your well-earned treasure.

A Cache of Cash on Cache *(cont.)*

Source 4

312 Cache Ave.

A Cache of Cash on Cache *(cont.)*

Name: _____

Part 1: Read each idea. Which source gives you this information? Fill in the correct bubble for each source. (Note: More than one bubble may be filled in for each idea.)

Information	Sources ➡	1	2	3	4
1. A treasure is hidden on Cache Ave.		○	○	○	○
2. The treasure is in the form of cash.		○	○	○	○
3. Four clues are needed to find the treasure.		○	○	○	○
4. The house on Cache Avenue has a swingset in the backyard.		○	○	○	○

Part 2: Fill in the bubble(s) next to the best answer(s) to each question.

5. In the title of this unit ("A Cache of Cash on Cache"), to what does the final *Cache* refer?

Ⓐ a hidden supply

Ⓑ the name of a street

Ⓒ a buried treasure

Ⓓ another word for *money*

6. In the fourth paragraph of Source 3, the author refers to a "natural object." Which of the following are natural objects?

Ⓐ tree

Ⓑ mailbox

Ⓒ doghouse

Ⓓ rosebushes

7. Based on Source 2, you know that the words *cash* and *cache* are _____.

Ⓐ synonyms

Ⓑ antonyms

Ⓒ homophones

Ⓓ homographs

8. Near the end of Source 1, the effect is that Kyle is out of breath as he tries to give some news to Kayla. What is the cause?

Ⓐ There is a hidden treasure.

Ⓑ There are four clues to find.

Ⓒ Kyle ran 10 blocks to Kayla's house.

Ⓓ Kayla knows the meaning of the word *cache*.

Part 3: Search "A Cache of Cash on Cache" to find one example of each of the following. Then write the number of the source in which you located this information.

9. a word meaning "four of something" _____ Source #: _____

10. a synonym for the word *flapped* _____ Source #: _____

A Cache of Cash on Cache *(cont.)*

Name: _____

Part 4: Refer back to the sources, and when possible, use complete sentences to answer these questions.

11. In Source 1, why does Kayla say, "It makes sense that a treasure would be hidden in that location"?

_____

_____

_____

_____

_____

12. Fill in the chart below with information about the clues given in Source 3. Use Source 4 to help you.

	Clue #1	Clue #2	Clue #3	Clue #4
Where was it located?				
Which letter was there?				

13. Answer these questions about the treasure on Cache Ave.

A. Where is the treasure hidden? _____

B. How do you know this? _____

_____

_____

C. How much is the treasure worth? _____

D. Write the quote from Source 3 that gives the information needed to answer the previous question.

_____

_____

_____

Seeing Eye to Eye

Read each source below. Then complete the activities on pages 67–68.

Source 1

Little Book of Literary Terms

idiom – a form of expression that has a figurative meaning but cannot be interpreted literally

"The two friends see eye to eye on most issues." (They do not *literally* look into each other's eyes in this example. This expression means that they agree on most things.)

irony – a figure of speech in which a phrase ends up meaning the exact opposite of what one would expect it to mean

page 6

Source 2

Tori and Tony stood on the sidewalk, waiting for the WALK sign. As a siren began to blare in the distance, Tori tightened her grip on her young son's hand. The siren grew louder, and then a vehicle could be seen. Red lights flashed along its roof.

Tony pointed at the hood of the emergency vehicle. "What's that word?" he shouted.

"It's the word *AMBULANCE*," his mother shouted back.

"No, it isn't. The first letter is an E. And it's written funny!"

Tori waited until the ambulance passed. Then in a quieter voice, she said, "I see why you'd say that. The word *ambulance* was spelled backwards. It's spelled that way so when drivers look into their rearview mirrors, they can see that the vehicle coming up behind them is an ambulance. This could be helpful if the driver can't hear the sirens."

Source 3

Cory and Rory are identical twins. They have the same blue eyes and the same thin nose. On each one, the left ear is slightly larger than its right counterpart. Cory and Rory each have the same brown hair, and they each part it to the right. They look the same, but they do not share the same opinions.

"The hardest thing to do in pro sports is hit a baseball," said Rory. "If you can get a hit just 33% of the time, you will be one of the all-time greats. Name another job where you can fail two-thirds of the time and still be among the best."

Cory scoffed at his brother. "Playing quarterback is the hardest thing to do. Try throwing a football to a precise spot 50 yards down the field, all while an incredibly fast 300-pound man is running straight at you, intending to knock you unconscious."

Cory continued, "Speaking of big, fast, aggressive things, you would agree that the hippopotamus is the most dangerous animal in the world, right?"

"No, it isn't!" countered Rory. "A Komodo dragon is a 10-foot-long lizard with sharp teeth, powerful jaws, and toxic saliva. Do you know how a lizard could grow to be so big? No one wants to fight it."

"That reminds me of that dragon movie we saw last week," said Cory. "Best movie ever!"

Rory groaned. "It had unbelievable characters, awful dialogue, and no plot!"

Cory stared at his identical twin. It was like looking into a mirror and seeing an exact copy of himself glaring back. He said, "You and I don't see eye to eye on much, do we?"

"I'd agree with that," smiled Rory.

Seeing Eye to Eye *(cont.)*

Name: _____

Part 1: Read each idea. Which person(s) from the sources does this describe? (Note: More than one bubble may be filled in for each idea.)

Information	Person ➡	Cory	Rory	Tony	Tori
1. This person is a twin.		○	○	○	○
2. This person is a son.		○	○	○	○
3. This person is a parent.		○	○	○	○
4. This person says, "No, it isn't."		○	○	○	○

Part 2: Fill in the bubble(s) next to the best answer(s) to each question.

5. Which of the following does Cory argue in favor of?

    Ⓐ hippopotamuses   Ⓒ the dragon movie

    Ⓑ Komodo dragons   Ⓓ baseball

6. In Source 2, it is implied that Tori "shouted" at her son because

    Ⓐ he was letting go of her hand.

    Ⓑ he was walking into the street.

    Ⓒ he was asking too many questions.

    Ⓓ she wanted to be heard over the siren noise.

7. Which word from the sources means "a thing whose function corresponds to that of another thing"?

    Ⓐ expression   Ⓒ counterpart

    Ⓑ dialogue   Ⓓ vehicle

8. In Source 3, is Rory's baseball math correct?

    Ⓐ Yes, to succeed 33% of the time would be to fail two-thirds of the time.

    Ⓑ No, to succeed 33% of the time would be to fail two-thirds of the time.

    Ⓒ No, because you cannot use percentages and fractions in the same equation.

    Ⓓ No, because football is harder to play than baseball.

Part 3: Search "Seeing Eye to Eye" to find one example of the following adjectives. Then write the number of the source in which you located this information.

    9. a synonym for "poisonous" _____ Source #: _____

    10. an antonym for "easygoing"_____ Source #: _____

Name: _____

Part 4: Refer back to the sources, and use complete sentences to answer these questions.

11. In the box below, write the word that Tony sees on the emergency vehicle in Source 2. Write it exactly as he sees it.

┌───┐
│   │
│   │
│   │
│   │
└───┘

12. The following lines appear near the end of Source 3: "Cory stared at his identical twin. It was like looking into a mirror and seeing an exact copy of himself glaring back." Taken literally, this statement could not be completely true. Why? Use information from another source to prove your point.

_____

_____

_____

_____

_____

_____

_____

13. Later in Source 3, one of the twins says, "You and I don't see eye to eye very much, do we?" Explain why this statement contains both an idiom and an example of irony.

_____

_____

_____

_____

_____

_____

_____

All Ears

Read each source below. Then complete the activities on pages 70–71.

Source 1

As my spacecraft touched down on Polypinnae, I thought back to my school days when I first read about this mysterious planet and its inhabitants. It had been decades since anyone from my planet had made contact with the Polypins.

Upon exiting my vehicle, I used my high-powered binoculars to observe a group of these two-foot-tall blue-green beings in the distance about 5,000 feet away. It was not their height or color, however, that most caught my eye. I knew from their planet's name that they would have many ears, but they appeared to be *all* ears. On each Polypin, I counted eleven ears of varying size. I could not see any mouths or eyes.

As I cleared my throat to call out to them, they seemed to recoil in pain. Into my megaphone, I announced, "I am from the planet—," but then stopped. The Polypins were hopping up and down in an agitated way. Under my breath, I muttered, "If only they would come closer."

One of the Polypins flapped its many ears and flew over to me. It whispered, "We are close enough. We can hear you from a mile away." It then retreated back to its group.

I put down my megaphone, and in a quieter voice said, "Forgive me, friends. I come in peace, and I bring urgent news. My people have unearthed a great threat that could adversely affect everyone in our galaxy cluster." The Polypins seemed to lose interest as I spoke. Many of them turned away.

I continued, "Please hear what I am about to say. My leaders have made it our planet's mission to warn our neighbors." My voice trailed off. Some of the Polypins were playing, others were lying down to sleep, and still others had simply flown away. All of them had stopped listening.

Source 2

Polypinnae

- located in Galaxy K7q4j
- the eleventh planet from Helio 592D
- discovered in the year 2326

named after its inhabitants (from the Greek root *poly* meaning "much" or "many" and the Latin word *pinnae* for "wings"; in zoology, *pinna* is the name given to the outer part of an animal's ear)

Source 3

Big Book of Literary Terms

hyperbole – extreme exaggeration

Example: I could hear his snoring from a mile away. (The snoring might be very loud, but not so loud that it could *literally* be heard from that great of a distance.)

idiom – an expression that has a figurative meaning and cannot be interpreted literally

Example: Joe said, "If you have something to say, I'm all ears." (Joe is not *literally* made up of only ears. Since ears are the organs associated with hearing/listening, Joe is saying that he is going to focus on listening to what the other person has to say.)

irony – a figure of speech in which a phrase ends up meaning the exact opposite of what one would expect it to mean

Name: _____

Part 1: Read each idea. Which source does it describe? Fill in the correct bubble for each source. (Note: More than one bubble may be filled in for each idea.)

Information Sources ➡	1	2	3
1. This source is written in first person.	○	○	○
2. This source contains dialogue.	○	○	○
3. This source describes an experience.	○	○	○
2. This source comes from a reference book.	○	○	○

Part 2: Fill in the bubble(s) next to the best answer(s) to each question.

5. Which of the sources are written in the genre of science fiction?

Ⓐ Source 1   Ⓒ Source 3

Ⓑ Source 2   Ⓓ all of the above

6. From Source 2, you can infer that zoology is the study of _____.

Ⓐ ears   Ⓒ animals

Ⓑ aliens   Ⓓ Polypins

7. Look at the following phrases from the sources. Which of these underlined words is being used as an adverb?

Ⓐ "a great threat that could <u>adversely</u> affect everyone"

Ⓑ "hopping up and down in an <u>agitated</u> way"

Ⓒ "and I bring <u>urgent</u> news"

Ⓓ "eleven ears of <u>varying</u> size"

8. In Source 1, when the Polypin says, "We can hear you from a mile away," it is

Ⓐ using hyperbole.   Ⓒ using irony.

Ⓑ using an idiom.   Ⓓ being literal.

Part 3: Search "All Ears" to find one example of each of the following. Then write the number of the source in which you located this information.

9. a word that means "discovered" or "uncovered" _____   Source #: _____

10. a word that contains the name of a real planet _____   Source #: _____

Name: _____

Part 4: Refer back to the sources, and use complete sentences to answer these questions.

11. Do you agree or disagree with this statement: The main character in Source 1 is familiar with the information given in Source 2? State your opinion and provide evidence from the sources to support your claim.

_____

_____

_____

_____

_____

_____

12. Use the format of a four-panel comic strip to summarize the events of Source 1. In at least one panel, be sure to include a drawing of a Polypin.

13. Taking into consideration the information given in Source 3, what is ironic about the Polypins?

_____

_____

_____

_____

_____

All Thumbs

Read each source below and on page 73. Then complete the activities on pages 74–75.

Source 1

"all thumbs"

idiom

Meaning: very awkward and clumsy, especially with one's hands

---

Source 2

Charley sat down at the old family computer. He used his right index finger to peck at the letters on the keyboard. Aunt Dee gasped. "Haven't they taught you how to type at school?" she asked. "You need to put your fingers on home row. And you must use *all* of your fingers, not just your pointer."

Charley laughed, "I have no idea what 'home row' is. This keyboard is a dinosaur! It's slowing me down. Nobody texts faster than me." To demonstrate, Charley pulled out his phone. His thumbs deftly darted across the tiny keys. "Done!"

Aunt Dee shook her head. "That's not typing."

Charley shrugged, "Just because you've always done something one way doesn't mean that's the best way to do it."

Source 3

Ms. Capps pointed at the diagram on the screen. "This is the traditional QWERTY keyboard. If you look at the top-left section of letters, you can see how this keyboard got its name. You may also notice that about half of the letters are shaded. These shaded letters are the ones that should be struck with the fingers of your left hand. The unshaded letters should be struck with the fingers of your right hand.

"The middle row, or 'home row' as it is known, is also very important. Before you begin to type, you should set your fingers on the keys that make up home row. The four fingers of your left hand go on the letters *a* (pinkie), *s* (ring), *d* (middle), and *f* (index). The four fingers of your right hand go on *j* (index), *k* (middle), *l* (ring), and *;* (pinkie). Your fingers can reach all of the other keys from this position. Your thumbs are used to strike the long space bar at the bottom center of your keyboard."

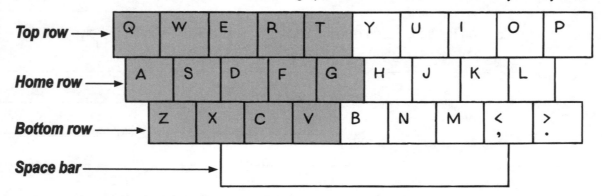

Source 4

All Thumbs, Indeed

by Maisy O'Day

I'll admit it: I cannot function without my mobile device. I rely on it to communicate with the world around me. All day long, I use my thumbs to type out texts, e-mails, and Internet addresses on its small screen. I make many errors.

This is *not* how I learned to type, you see. I learned to type on a large keyboard, with my fingers resting on home row. Those lessons from long ago did not prepare me for typing on my smartphone as I walk along a busy street, juggling a bottle of water and a frosted cronut.

Who or what can I blame for this difficult life I lead? QWERTY, that's who. QWERTY is the name given to the style of keyboard we've all been using since forever (actually, since 1875). A QWERTY-style keyboard is named after the six consecutive letters at the top left of the keyboard. That style, with that arrangement of letters, is a throwback to the time when we used clunky typewriters and all of our fingers to type. Does QWERTY still make sense in today's world?

Researchers say it doesn't. They say it's not very efficient. Too many of the most common letters are typed with the left hand, and our fingers need to jump around too much to form common words. Thankfully, these researchers have aimed to make our lives easier by creating a solution: the KALQ system.

In 2013, the KALQ keyboard was introduced. Research shows that it allows people to thumb-type 34% faster than the QWERTY. Here's how:

- ☞ Each thumb is used almost the same amount of time. This allows the opposite thumb to get into position while the typing thumb is at work.

- ☞ You alternate the use of thumbs much more often. Over 60% of the time, the next key you strike will be with the opposite thumb than the key you just struck.

- ☞ Your thumbs have to travel less distance.

- ☞ The spacebars are located in the center for each thumb.

- ☞ The vowels (except for *y*) are located very close to one another.

the split-screen KALQ keyboard

left-hand keys   *right-hand keys*

Today, I downloaded KALQ onto my phone. I gave it a try. My typing was sloppier than ever! Of course, I'm not accustomed to the new layout, so I spent a lot of time looking at the screen and searching for letters. Researchers say that it takes about 8 hours to learn the new layout. Who has that kind of time? Ok, that's not a good excuse, but I think I should be more grateful for QWERTY. I guess there's a reason why it's endured for 140 years.

Name: _____

Part 1: Read each description. Does it describe the QWERTY typing system or the KALQ typing system? Fill in the correct bubble(s) for each source. If it describes both systems, fill in both bubbles.

Description	Typing System ➡	QWERTY	KALQ
1. This system is named for a group of consecutive letters on its keypad.		○	○
2. This system has the user strike the space bar with his/her thumb.		○	○
3. This system has the user strike the *e* key with his/her right hand.		○	○
4. This system has the user strike the *s* key with his/her left hand.		○	○

Part 2: Fill in the bubble next to the best answer to each question.

5. When using correct typing form on a QWERTY keyboard, which of the letters in the "word" *qwerty* is not struck using a finger on the left hand?

  Ⓐ q

  Ⓑ w

  Ⓒ t

  Ⓓ y

6. What is another name for the pointer finger?

  Ⓐ index

  Ⓑ middle

  Ⓒ ring

  Ⓓ pinkie

7. In Source 1, Charley says "Nobody texts faster than me." This sentence does not use correct grammar. Which of the following would be more correct?

  Ⓐ "No body texts faster than me."

  Ⓑ "Nobody texts fastest than me."

  Ⓒ "Nobody texts faster then me."

  Ⓓ "Nobody texts faster than I."

8. Which key is mentioned in the text of Source 3 but not shown in the illustration?

  Ⓐ [,] Ⓑ [;] Ⓒ [:] Ⓓ [?]

Part 3: Search "All Thumbs" to find examples of compound words with the following meanings. Then write the number of the source in which you located each word.

9. "copied data from one computer to another" _____ Source #: _____

10. "a thing from an earlier time period" _____ Source #: _____

Part 4: Use complete sentences to answer these questions.

11. In Source 2, Charley says, "This keyboard is a dinosaur!" What does he mean by this, and how is this an example of metaphor (a figure of speech in which an unrelated word or phrase is used to describe an object)?

_____

_____

_____

_____

_____

12. Later in Source 2, Charley says, "Just because you've always done something one way doesn't mean that's the best way to do it." Do you think a new way of typing is needed to keep up with today's technology? Give reasons to explain why you think the old way is better or why a new way is needed.

_____

_____

_____

_____

_____

13. Source 4 is in the form of a web log, or *blog*. What is the central idea of the first two paragraphs of Source 4? What details does the blog's author use to express this idea?

_____

_____

_____

_____

_____

_____

_____

All the Same to Me

Read each source below. Then complete the activities on pages 77–78.

Source 1

People think my kind will only eat one thing: ants. Where I live in the South American country of Brazil, the local people call us *tamandua*. That word means "catcher of ants." I'm told that people in other countries simply call us "anteaters." No wonder there is a misunderstanding about our diet. Well, ants are not *all* that I eat. I also love eating termites! See, I'm not *that* picky.

Ants and termites are not the same things. In fact, do you know which animals most often terrorize termites? Ants! Ants invade termite mounds and aim to destroy them and kill everybody inside. In contrast, I am very careful when I visit a termite mound. First, I use my sharp claws to neatly make a hole in the mound. Next, I use my long, thin tongue to quickly feed on a few thousand insects. (I have to admit, my tongue is pretty awesome. It's covered with backward-curving spines, and it's coated with sticky saliva.) Then I leave before I get stung or bitten too much.

When I leave, I am careful to leave the mound intact. It's the least I can do, since those termites go to so much trouble to build their beautiful homes. Besides, I need to visit a lot of termite mounds and anthills each day. If I destroyed every home I came across, I couldn't go back and feed again when I got hungry. It's a win-win situation for me and the insects who live in my neighborhood.

Source 2

excerpt from *All About Insects*
Chapter 27: Termites

Although termites are often called "white ants," these two types of animals are not related. While both are insects—and as such have three segments, six legs, etc.—there are some obvious differences in the look of the two animals. First, a termite's antennae are straight, while an ant's antennae are elbowed, or bent. Another difference can be seen in their bodies. An ant's body grows very narrow between the thorax (second segment) and the abdomen (third segment). A termite's body is much broader where the two segments connect.

Ants and termites both build and live in nests, either underground or above the ground. Both form colonies in which there are workers who build the nest and soldiers who protect it from invaders. We learned in the previous chapter that ant colonies are made up mostly of females, with the males only living a short time and only needed to do specific short-term jobs. In contrast, a termite colony is formed by a king and a queen, and males are important members of a termite society.

Termites often build their nests underground or inside trees or woody environments. Some build above-ground mounds that can reach as high as nearly 30 feet tall.

Source 3

excerpt from *All About Anteaters*
Chapter 4: The Animal's Diet

As their name implies, anteaters eat ants. They also eat termites. Together, these two insects form the majority of the anteater's diet. Anteaters live in the grasslands and wet forests of Central or South America, where these insects are plentiful.

Since anteaters have poor eyesight but a keen sense of smell, they locate a food source by its scent. Once it finds an anthill or termite mound, the anteater uses its razor-sharp, four-inch claws to tear open a hole in the nest. Once the hole is made, the animal sticks its elongated snout into the hole and uses its narrow, two-foot-long tongue to extract insects. The anteater must eat quickly. Ants and termites bite and sting. An anteater can lap up thousands of insects in about 1 minute. Once again, the anteater's specialized tongue makes this possible. An anteater can rapidly flick its tongue at a rate of about 160 times per minute!

Name: _____

Part 1: Read each idea. Which source gives you this information? Fill in the correct bubble for each source. (Note: More than one bubble may be filled in for each idea.)

Information	Sources ➡	1	2	3
1. Anteaters have poor eyesight.		○	○	○
2. Anteaters have sharp claws.		○	○	○
3. Anteaters live in South America.		○	○	○
4. Both ants and anteaters invade termite mounds.		○	○	○

Part 2: Fill in the bubble next to the best answer to each question.

5. Which of the sources is most clearly a work of fiction?

Ⓐ Source 1

Ⓑ Source 2

Ⓒ Source 3

Ⓓ All are nonfiction.

6. What is the subject of Chapter 26 of *All About Insects*?

Ⓐ ants

Ⓑ anteaters

Ⓒ termites

Ⓓ termite mounds

7. In the first paragraph of Source 1, why are the words *all* and *that* in italic (slanted) type?

Ⓐ to show that they are nouns

Ⓑ to put emphasis on them

Ⓒ to show how anteaters talk and think

Ⓓ because they start with the letters *a* and *t* (like *ants* and *termites*)

8. Who is most likely the "Me" in the unit title "All the Same to Me"?

Ⓐ the author of *All About Anteaters*

Ⓑ the author of *All About Insects*

Ⓒ the queen in an ant colony

Ⓓ the anteater in Source 1

Part 3: Search "All the Same to Me" to find hyphenated terms with the following meanings. Then write the number of the source in which you located this information.

9. "temporary occupations" _____ Source #: _____

10. "a result that pleases everyone" _____ Source #: _____

All the Same to Me (cont.)

Name: _____

Part 4: Refer back to the sources, and use complete sentences to answer these questions.

11. Does the picture to the right show an ant or a termite? Use evidence from at least one of the sources to support your answer.

_____

_____

_____

_____

_____

12. Using more than one source, name at least four ways in which an anteater's tongue is "specialized" to help it eat ants and termites.

_____

_____

_____

_____

_____

_____

_____

_____

13. Most animals do not have names that are as obvious or practical as an anteater's. What if all animals were named based on what they ate or how they looked? Think of a common animal, and give it a more practical name. Explain why you chose this name for this animal.

_____

_____

_____

_____

_____

_____

_____

_____

Not the Same Thing

Read each source below. Then complete the activities on pages 80–81.

Source 1

In chemistry, the pH scale is used to measure how acidic or basic a substance is. The scale goes from 0–14. Substances with pH measurements of less than 7 are *acidic*. Those with measurements higher than 7 are *basic*. A solution with a measurement of 7 is considered *neutral*.

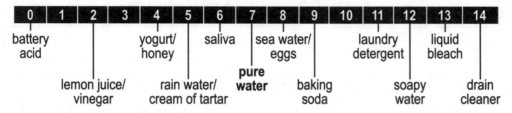

0	1	2	3	4	5	6	7	8	9	10	11	12	13	14

battery acid — lemon juice/vinegar — yogurt/honey — rain water/cream of tartar — saliva — **pure water** — sea water/eggs — baking soda — laundry detergent — soapy water — liquid bleach — drain cleaner

Source 2

Baker Bob's Tips for Success #26 Make Your Own Baking Powder!

If there's one thing we bakers know, it's that it is crucial to follow the recipe. Precise measurements must be used, and some ingredients can never be replaced! For example, what can you do if you run out of baking powder? Maybe you could just use baking soda instead? They are the same thing, right? Wrong!

Here's a quick science lesson: Chemically speaking, baking soda is a *base* ingredient. Because of this, it needs an *acidic* ingredient (yogurt, honey, buttermilk, etc.) to help it release gas. When baking soda is combined with moisture and an acidic ingredient, a chemical reaction occurs. This produces bubbles of gas (carbon dioxide) that expand under high temperatures (as in an oven). This makes cakes, breads, and other baked goods rise as they bake. In contrast, baking powder already has an acidic ingredient in it. Which one you use—baking soda or baking powder—depends on the other ingredients in your recipe.

So in order to turn your baking soda into baking powder, you need to add an acid to it. Enter cream of tartar. Many of you have this handy ingredient in your cupboards. When it is mixed properly with baking soda—two parts cream of tartar to one part baking soda—a homemade baking powder can be concocted. And that, my fellow bakers, is today's Tip for Success.

Source 3

Dear Mia,

Here's that biscuit recipe you asked for. I'm just giving it to you off the top of my head, but I don't think I've forgotten anything. It's super simple, and you know these biscuits will be a big hit at your dinner party!

Love, Mama

Ingredients

- 2 cups flour
- 1 tablespoon baking soda
- 1 teaspoon salt
- $\frac{2}{3}$ cup of milk
- $\frac{1}{3}$ cup of oil

Directions

1. Preheat oven to 450°F.

2. Combine dry ingredients in a bowl. Add in the two wet ingredients to moisten. Gently knead dough about 10 times.

3. Roll out dough until it is about $\frac{3}{4}$" thick. Cut into six biscuits.

4. Put biscuits on a baking sheet and bake until golden brown. Takes about 12 minutes.

Not the Same Thing (cont.)

Name: _____

Part 1: Read each idea. Which source gives you this information? Fill in the correct bubble for each source. (Note: More than one bubble may be filled in for each idea.)

Information	Sources ➡	1	2	3
1. Cream of tartar is an acidic substance.		○	○	○
2. Buttermilk is an acidic substance.		○	○	○
3. Pure water is a neutral ingredient.		○	○	○
4. Ovens can reach temperatures of over 400°F.		○	○	○

Part 2: Fill in the bubble next to the best answer to each question.

5. What does the author of the note in Source 3 mean when she says she is giving the recipe "off the top of her head"?

Ⓐ She keeps it under her hat.

Ⓑ She is reciting it from memory.

Ⓒ It is her very best recipe.

Ⓓ She is getting it from a website on the Internet.

6. The author of Source 2 uses the word *crucial*. Which of the following actions would be the most crucial for you to do as soon as you are done baking biscuits?

Ⓐ Turn off the oven.

Ⓑ Cut the dough into biscuits.

Ⓒ Place biscuits on a nice dish.

Ⓓ Wash all dirty bowls and utensils.

7. For the biscuit recipe in Source 3, what is the total amount of wet ingredients needed?

Ⓐ $\frac{2}{3}$ cup

Ⓑ $\frac{3}{4}$ cup

Ⓒ 1 cup

Ⓓ $1\frac{1}{3}$ cups

8. In Source 3, Mia's mother does not write down every step that must be taken when baking biscuits. Some steps are implied, or obvious. In the fourth direction of the recipe, which step is implied?

Ⓐ Put biscuits on a baking sheet.

Ⓑ Put biscuits into the oven.

Ⓒ Bake biscuits until they are golden brown.

Ⓓ Bake biscuits for about 12 minutes.

Part 3: Search "Not the Same Thing" to find one example of each of the following. Then write the number of the source in which you located this information.

9. a two-syllable compound word _____ Source #: _____

10. a three-syllable compound word _____ Source #: _____

Not the Same Thing *(cont.)*

Name: _____

Part 4: Refer back to the sources, and use complete sentences to answer these questions.

11. Imagine that you need to bake an enormous cake, and you're all out of baking powder. You do, however, have plenty of baking soda and cream of tartar. In all, you need 12 teaspoons of baking powder. How can you use what you have to make what you need? Give the exact amounts of each ingredient, and explain how you came up with your answer.

_____

_____

_____

_____

_____

_____

12. Mia's dinner party turned out great, except for her biscuits. They were a disaster. They were flat and hard, and they did not have the correct texture. What must have happened? Did Mia do something wrong, or was her mother's recipe to blame? Give evidence to support your answer.

_____

_____

_____

_____

_____

13. A common science experiment is to create a model-sized volcano with erupting "lava." To make the "lava" erupt, you place baking soda inside the volcano and then pour vinegar over the baking soda. Why does this work? Why does the baking soda and vinegar solution erupt out of the volcano? Use what you have learned in Sources 1–3 to explain your answer.

_____

_____

_____

_____

_____

Chasing the Cheese

Read each source below and on page 83. Then complete the activities on pages 84–86.

Source 1

To	mama1972@zmail.net
From	alliegater2002@zmail.net
Subject	IT'S OFFICIAL!
Date	April 12, 2026

Hello Mom!

It's official: I just bought the plane tickets. Other Allison and I are set to go to England in late May. Yes, that means we are going to compete in this year's Cheese Rolling Contest!

I know how you feel about it, but I'm eagerly anxious to do this. (Other Allison is, too!) It will be a thrill to compete in a contest that has been held for 200 years. That's a lot of tradition, and I'll be a part of it. Maybe some day, a child of mine can take part in this event, too, and it will become a family tradition!

Oh, and if I win, I promise to share some of the cheese prize with you. After all, I can't eat 30 pounds of cheese by myself!

Love always,
Your Allison

Source 2

To	alliegater2002@zmail.net
From	mama1972@zmail.net
Subject	Re: IT'S OFFICIAL!
Date	April 12, 2026

Oh Allison, please be careful! I just looked up the Cooper's Hill Cheese Rolling contest on my computer, and I'm genuinely concerned. This event is very dangerous. A lot of people get injured. Have you seen a picture of the hill? Does it really look safe to you? Here, click on this link:

www.images.com/coopershill3756

Other Allison's mother and I will be awfully worried. BUT I know that you two are all grown up and have to make your own choices. Just please wear some padding, and remember that "Slow and steady wins the race."

What date will the contest be held this year? Where will you be staying?

Love,
Your worried Mom

Source 3

Image Search results for "Cooper's Hill Cheese Rolling"

www.images.com/coopershill3756

**spectators await the start of
a race at Cooper's Hill**

www.images.com/coopershill3765

**a winner proudly displays
her prize**

Source 4

Pine Bluff Press

Sunday, May 31, 2026   Page 6

Two Friends, One Cheese

What would you do for a big chunk of cheese? Would you spend hundreds of dollars and travel thousands of miles? Would you race down an impossibly steep hill, risking injury with every unsteady step?

That's what two local women were willing to do. Allison Gates and Allison Wells have been friends since preschool. The two 23-year-olds have lived in Pine Bluff all their lives and have shared many things, including a taste for adventure. Last year, the pair climbed Avalanche Peak in Yellowstone National Park. This year they decided to go *down* a mountain instead of up one. They decided to compete in the world-famous Cooper's Hill Cheese Rolling contest.

Cooper's Hill is a very steep hill located in Gloucester, England. Each year on the last Monday in May, a daring group of men and women chase a large, round cheese as it tumbles down this hill. The people who chase the cheese end up tumbling down the hill, as well. It is almost impossible to stay on one's feet, and this is what can turn a fun event into a painful one. Injuries occur every year. Few runners escape without scrapes and bruises. Broken bones and concussions are not uncommon. In 1997 there were so many injuries that the event was cancelled the following year.

This leads us back to Allison Wells. She was one of the unfortunate runners who took home something other than a cheese. About 10 yards into her trek down the hill, Allison took a bad step and slipped. Her left leg buckled. This sent her plunging end over end down the hill. When she finally came to a stop, she knew her ankle was severely sprained. "It was a nasty spill," she said. "I was lucky I didn't break anything. And then I saw Allison cross the finish line, and I forgot all about the pain in my leg."

Cheese Rolling—Fast Facts

▲ The tradition was first written about in 1826. It may have been held before then, however.

▲ There are three men's races and one women's race each year. The winner of each race receives a cheese.

▲ The cheeses used and given as prizes weigh between 7–9 pounds.

▲ Each year, about 5,000 people gather at Cooper's Hill to watch the event.

▲ Several spectators are injured each year, either from a rolling cheese or from falling down the hill.

▲ The event was not held in 1998, 2001, or 2003.

Her friend Allison Gates did indeed make it to the finish line. She finished first and became one of four runners to take home a cheese that day. "I can't believe I made it down the hill in one piece, let alone that I won! I only wish Allison hadn't gotten hurt. I was truly upset when I saw the medics working on her leg. I'm glad she's okay."

Doctors have assured Allison Wells that she will be fully healed in about three months. She'll be on her feet and ready to go next summer when the duo plans their next adventure.

Chasing the Cheese *(cont.)*

Name: _____

Part 1: Read each idea. Which source gives you this information? Fill in the correct bubble for each source. (Note: More than one bubble may be filled in for each idea.)

Information	Sources ➡	1	2	3	4
1. A cheese-rolling contest takes place in England.		○	○	○	○
2. A cheese-rolling contest takes place on Cooper's Hill.		○	○	○	○
3. Spectators gather to watch the contest.		○	○	○	○
4. Winners takes home cheese as a prize.		○	○	○	○

Part 2: Fill in the bubble next to the best answer to each question.

5. In her quote in the newspaper article, which synonym did Allison Wells use for the word *fall*?

Ⓐ slip　　　　　　　　　　Ⓒ tumble

Ⓑ spill　　　　　　　　　　Ⓓ plunge

6. Near the end of Source 2, the e-mailer asks, "What date will the contest be held this year?" What is the answer to that question? Use clues from Source 4 to help you.

Ⓐ May 24, 2026　　　　　　Ⓒ May 30, 2026

Ⓑ May 25, 2026　　　　　　Ⓓ May 31, 2026

7. The word *hyperbole* means "extreme exaggeration." About what does Allison use hyperbole in her e-mail to her mother?

Ⓐ how many years the contest has been held

Ⓑ how many people are injured each year

Ⓒ how much the cheese prize weighs

Ⓓ how much it costs to fly to England

8. All of the following phrases from the sources have to do with anxiety and/or worry. Which one of these phrases has a positive connotation (association)?

Ⓐ eagerly anxious　　　　　Ⓒ awfully worried

Ⓑ genuinely concerned　　　Ⓓ truly upset

Part 3: Search "Chasing Cheese" to find one example of each of the following. Then write the number of the source in which you located this information.

9. a possessive proper noun _____ Source #: _____

10. an adverb with four syllables _____ Source #: _____

Chasing the Cheese *(cont.)*

Name: _____

Part 4: Refer back to the sources, and use complete sentences to answer these questions.

11. Compare and contrast the two sources that are presented in the form of e-mails. What are the tones of the e-mails? On which part of the contest does each author focus?

_____

_____

_____

_____

_____

12. Analyze the structure of the newspaper article in Source 4. Describe how each part contributes to the whole.

Paragraph 1   How does it begin? _____

What is the purpose of this paragraph? _____

_____

Paragraph 2   How does it begin? _____

What is the purpose of this paragraph? _____

_____

Paragraph 3   How does it begin? _____

What is the purpose of this paragraph? _____

_____

Paragraph 4   How does it begin? _____

What is the purpose of this paragraph? _____

_____

Paragraph 5   How does it begin? _____

What is the purpose of this paragraph? _____

_____

Sidebar   In the article, what is the purpose of this feature?

_____

_____

Name: _____

Part 4 *(cont.):*

13. Imagine that you are one of the Allisons writing an e-mail to her mother. Use the information given in the sources. Follow this structure:

✳ **Paragraph 1:** Explain that you have returned from England.

✳ **Paragraph 2:** Explain what it was like to participate in the contest.

✳ **Paragraph 3:** Explain what happened to you during the contest.

✳ **Paragraph 4:** Explain what happened to the other Allison in the contest.

✳ **Paragraph 5:** Explain what you and the other Allison plan to do next year.

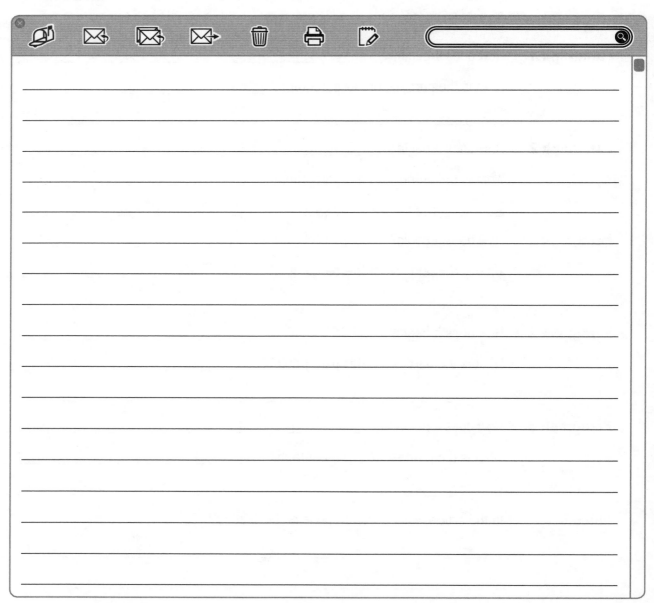

Two Singular Creatures

Read each source below and on page 88. Then complete the activities on pages 89–91.

Source 1

singular
(sing yoo lur)
adjective

1. remarkable, extraordinary
2. denoting one (as in grammar)
3. being the only one of its kind

Source 2

Grammar Tips!

A **singular noun** names one person, animal, place, thing, or idea.

A **plural noun** names more than one person, animal, place, thing, or idea.

For most nouns (with plurals formed regularly):

✳ Add *s* to most nouns to make them plural.

> **Examples: dog — dogs   worm — worms**

✳ Add *es* to words that end in *s*, *ch*, *sh*, *x*, and *z*.

> **Examples: bus — buses   dish — dishes**

For nouns ending in *y*:

✳ If the word ends with a vowel followed by *y*, just add *s*.

> **Examples: day — days   monkey — monkeys**

✳ If the word ends with a consonant followed by *y*, change the *y* to *i*, and add *es*.

> **Examples: fly — flies   penny — pennies**

For nouns ending in *f* or *fe*:

✳ In most cases, change the *f* or *fe* to *v* and add *es*.

> **Examples: leaf — leaves   knife — knives**

For other nouns (with plurals formed irregularly):

✳ Some words are the same in singular and plural form.

> **Examples: fish — fish   sheep — sheep**

✳ Some words are formed irregularly.

> **Examples: foot — feet   child — children**

Source 3

The **star-nosed mole** is a small mammal found in the northeastern part of North America. It can grow to about 8 inches in length; and it has a long tail, water-repellant fur, and 44 teeth. What really sets this animal apart, though, is its nose. This mole's snout, or nose, is ringed by 11 pairs of pink, fleshy appendages.

Because the mole is nearly blind, it uses its snout — which is covered with about 25,000 tiny sensory receptors — to gather information about its environment. Its diet consists mostly of worms, insects, and crustaceans. With its snout, it finds these food sources and gobbles them up quickly. In

fact, evidence suggests that the star-nosed mole is the world's fastest-eating mammal. Within 8 *milliseconds*, it can decide if a particle of food is edible or not. This is about as fast as a signal to the brain can travel. Within about 120 milliseconds, it can completely consume its meal. Star-nosed mole mothers probably never tell their children, "Slow down and chew your food!"

> **What Does It Mean?**
>
> **appendage** (noun)
> on animals, an anatomical part that sticks out from a larger part

Source 4

In the eastern region of Australia there lives a very unique animal. This animal has the tail of a beaver and the fur of an otter. It also has the bill and webbed feet of a duck. It's an expert swimmer, and it gathers its food by scooping up worms and crustaceans as it swims. It doesn't eat in the water, however. It stores food in its cheek pouches until it gets on land. When it leaves the water, the webbing on its feet retracts to bare its knuckles. It walks on these knuckles. Also, this animal doesn't have any teeth, so it picks up pieces of gravel in its mouth and uses the gravel to crush its food. If this animal is attacked, it has on each of its back feet a special spur that can inject a very venomous poison into its enemy. This strange animal is a mammal, but it lays eggs. Every other mammal, with the exception of a few anteaters, gives birth to live young. This amazing animal is the platypus, and it is absolutely one-of-a-kind.

Two Singular Creatures (cont.)

Name: _____

Part 1: Read each idea. Which source gives you this information? Fill in the correct bubble for each source. (Note: More than one bubble may be filled in for each idea.)

Information	Sources ➡	1	2	3	4
1. In grammar, *singular* means "one."		○	○	○	○
2. The plural of *worm* is *worms*.		○	○	○	○
3. The plural of *child* is *children*.		○	○	○	○
4. The platypus is not the fastest-eating mammal.		○	○	○	○

Part 2: Fill in the bubble next to the best answer to each question.

5. Which of these is not something that a platypus and a star-nosed mole have in common?

Ⓐ Both are mammals.

Ⓑ Both have appendages.

Ⓒ Both eat crustaceans.

Ⓓ Both lay eggs.

6. The plural of *platypus* is formed regularly. What is the plural of *platypus*?

Ⓐ platypus

Ⓑ platypuses

Ⓒ platypusses

Ⓓ platypi

7. How many total appendages does a star-nosed mole have on its snout?

Ⓐ 11

Ⓑ 22

Ⓒ 44

Ⓓ 120

8. A sidebar is an additional source of information that is included within or alongside a main article. Which source contains a sidebar?

Ⓐ Source 1

Ⓑ Source 2

Ⓒ Source 3

Ⓓ Source 4

Part 3: Search Sources 3 and 4 of "Two Singular Creatures" to find one example of each of the following. Then write the number of the source in which you located this information.

9. plural word that was formed by adding *es* _____ Source #: _____

10. plural word that was formed irregularly _____ Source #: _____

Name: _____

Part 4: Refer back to the sources, and use complete sentences to answer these questions.

11. Source 3 and Source 4 each give reports on specific animals. Think about how these two reports are written and structured. What are two main ways in which they are written and structured differently?

_____

_____

_____

_____

_____

In your opinion, which report is written or structured in a way that is more effective or interesting? Explain your answer.

_____

_____

_____

_____

12. Look at this statement: *The star-nosed mole is a singular animal.* Using each of the three definitions given in Source 1, explain how this statement is true.

_____

_____

_____

_____

_____

_____

_____

Two Singular Creatures *(cont.)*

Name: _____

Part 4 *(cont.):*

13. A *hybrid* is something made up of different parts from different things. The platypus is an unusual animal that could be called a hybrid since it seems to be made up of parts of other animals.

Using your imagination and your knowledge of animals, combine parts of several animals to create a new hybrid creature.

In the box . . .

✮ Draw a picture of your creation.

✮ Label each part of the new animal.

On the lines . . .

✮ Write a short report about the animal.

✮ Use the style and structure of either Source 3 or Source 4 to write your report.

Appropriately Named

Read each source below and on page 93. Then complete the activities on pages 94–95.

Source 1

I love words. Big words, little words—they're all fascinating as far as I'm concerned. And I love playing word games. It seemed like nobody else did, but then I met Eva. Her vocabulary is very impressive. We became fast friends.

Eva and I do this thing we like to call "Eva and Evan's Difficult and Diurnal Word Tournament." As the name suggests, we play this game every day. (It's an inside joke, too, because I didn't know the word *diurnal* until Eva used it in a sentence one day.) Basically, one of us comes up with an idea for a word game, and then the other one of us has to complete it. Most games contain a little twist that makes them extra impossible.

Today's game came courtesy of Eva. She sent me a word, and then I had to come up with one synonym and one antonym for that word. The catch was that each synonym and antonym had to start with the same letter as the original word. And I had to do this for the entire alphabet!

She started, of course, with the letter *a*. The word was *alert*. No problem. In fact, I was cruising along all the way to the letter *e*. That's when the game came to an abrupt end.

The front door of my house burst open, and in rushed Mom. Amid the jangling of keys and the crinkling of reusable bags, I could hear Mom calling "Evan!" I already knew what she was going to say. "I need help putting away the groceries, and then it's time for dinner."

I guess it was appropriate then that I had just written the word *ephemeral*. On this day, "Eva and Evan's Difficult and Diurnal Word Tournament" did not last long.

Source 2

Eva and Evan's
Difficult and Diurnal
Word Tournament for May 12, 2017

Letter	Word	Synonym	Antonym
A	alert	aware	asleep
B	boring	bland	bold
C	careful	cautious	careless
D	dry	dehydrated	damp
E	eternal	everlasting	ephemeral
F			
G			
H			

mayfly

Mayflies are insects that are classified scientifically as *Ephemeroptera*. This word combines two Greek roots:

* *ephemeros* (meaning "short-lived")
* *pteron* (meaning "wing")

These insects live in or near fresh water, and are in some ways related to dragonflies.

Mayflies, or *Ephemeroptera*, have a unique lifespan. The young of this species may live up to a year in fresh water, but it is from the adults that this insect gets its name. Adult mayflies live for a very short time. At most, they live for about a day, while some live for only a few hours. Adult mayflies stay alive just long enough to mate.

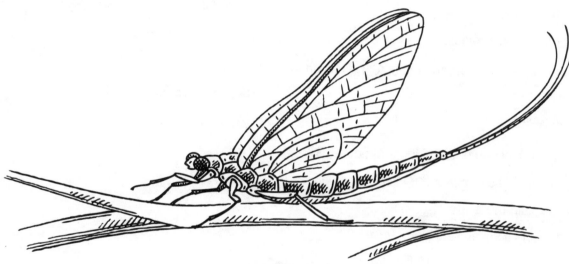

Only adult mayflies have wings.

The insect's anatomy ensures that it cannot survive for long periods of time. For example, an adult mayfly's mouthparts are vestigial, and its digestive system is filled with only air. Also, most of its legs are useless.

All of the adult mayflies in a population tend to hatch at the same time. For one or two days, large numbers of mayflies can be seen in one area. An enormous number of mayflies hatch each June along the Tisza River in Serbia and Hungary. This event is known as "Tisza blooming," and it is a tourist attraction.

What Does It Mean?

When used to describe body parts on animals, the word *vestigial* (veh-STI-jee-ul) refers to something that once served a function but no longer does.

Appropriately Named *(cont.)*

Name: _____

Part 1: Follow the rules of Eva's game and fill in the missing blanks in the chart below.

	Letter	Word	Synonym	Antonym
1.	m	massive	mammoth	
2.	r	regular	routine	
3.	s	soiled	stained	
4.	u	unique		

Part 2: Fill in the bubble next to the best answer to each question.

5. If an extinct animal is called a *pterosaur*, you would know from the Greek root in its name that

   Ⓐ it has wings.

   Ⓑ it has vestigial wings.

   Ⓒ it only lives for a short time.

   Ⓓ it lives near fresh water.

6. From the information given in Source 1, you can infer that the word *diurnal* means

   Ⓐ "difficult."

   Ⓑ "daily."

   Ⓒ "dehydrated."

   Ⓓ "ephemeral."

7. What is the function of the sidebar in Source 3?

   Ⓐ to explain the origin of the mayfly's name

   Ⓑ to explain the anatomy of mayflies

   Ⓒ to define a vocabulary word

   Ⓓ to tell how long adult mayflies live

8. The text in Source 3 states, "an adult mayfly's mouthparts are vestigial, and its digestive system is filled with only air." What can you infer from this statement?

   Ⓐ Adult mayflies only live for 24 hours.

   Ⓑ Adult mayflies have small mouths.

   Ⓒ Adult mayflies do not eat food.

   Ⓓ Adult mayflies all hatch at the same time.

Part 3: Search "Appropriately Named" to find one example of each of the following. Then write the number of the source in which you located this information.

9. a word describing a sound _____ Source #: _____

10. an adverb with six syllables _____ Source #: _____

Appropriately Named *(cont.)*

Name: _____

Part 4: Refer back to the sources, and use complete sentences to answer these questions.

11. The title of this unit is "Appropriately Named." Explain how this title applies to the game the characters play in Source 1.

_____

_____

_____

_____

_____

_____

12. Now explain how the title of this unit applies to *Ephemeroptera*, the scientific name given to mayflies. In doing so, examine each part of the name.

_____

_____

_____

_____

_____

_____

13. Imagine that the narrator of Source 1 is reading Source 3. Using what you know about Evan and what he tells us about himself, explain which part or parts of Source 3 he might find most interesting? Explain your choice(s).

_____

_____

_____

_____

_____

_____

_____

Into and Out of Thin Air

Read each source below. Then complete the activities on pages 97–99.

Source 1

"thin air" idioms

1. into thin air

Idiom: "vanish into thin air" (also, "disappear into thin air")

Meaning: to disappear, never to be seen again

2. out of thin air

Idiom: "appear out of thin air"

Meaning: suddenly and mysteriously appear

Source 2

The Water Cycle

Mr. Tanner's Class
Adams Elementary School, Room 6

Water does not come to Earth from other places. The water on Earth has always been here. It constantly gets used and reused. This is possible because of the water cycle. Water is always on the move. It moves from one place to another and from one form (solid, liquid, gas) to another.

There are four main stages of the water cycle:

1. Evaporation — During this stage, heat from the Sun causes water (in oceans, lakes, etc.) to evaporate (turn from a liquid into a gas). This gas is called water vapor, and it rises into the sky.

2. Condensation — As the water vapor in the air cools, it turns back into water droplets. The droplets form clouds in the sky.

3. Precipitation — As the droplets in the sky continue to condense, they become too heavy. It is called precipitation when the water falls back to the ground. It does this in many forms: rain, snow, sleet, hail.

4. Collection — When water falls to the ground, some of it ends up on land, where it nourishes plants and animals. The rest runs off the land and collects in oceans, lakes, rivers, and other bodies of water.

Source 3

Peter Tanner was in a panic. It was his first week on the job as a teacher at Adams Elementary, and his students were staring at him. He thought he had prepared well for his science lesson. However, when he went to open his computer file on the water cycle, he saw that all of the artwork was missing. The visuals seemed to have vanished into thin air.

The previous evening, Peter had painstakingly drawn clouds, raindrops, and all of the other elements that illustrated just how the water cycle works. He had scanned them into his computer. Everything was there when he went to sleep last night, and now *poof*—it was all gone. How could this happen? How would his students understand the concept of the water cycle if there were no visuals to go with the words? Peter wiped a bead of sweat from his brow and made a split-second decision. Instead of interrupting class to redo his presentation, he began to teach the four main stages of the water cycle. He decided that he would ask his students to draw the illustrations based on the descriptions he provided.

Source 4

I sighed and got busy searching the new teacher's computer for the "lost" artwork. I knew those files had to be somewhere. Data doesn't just disappear into thin air. Don't get me wrong—these teachers at Adams Elementary are great with kids, and they know their multiplication tables and dates in history. Technology is another story. Most of the teachers at this school are not exactly experts when it comes to computers. They hit the wrong button and unintentionally delete something, and then the principal calls me in to help find it. I can retrieve most any file. Things rarely get *completely* lost. I know where to look. Then it appears as if I pull the missing data out of thin air, but really it is hiding in plain sight the whole time.

Into and Out of Thin Air (cont.)

Name: _____

Part 1: Read each idea. Which source gives you this information? Fill in the correct bubble for each source. (Note: More than one bubble may be filled in for each idea.)

Information	Sources ➡	1	2	3	4
1. Condensation is a part of the water cycle.		○	○	○	○
2. Clouds are a part of the water cycle.		○	○	○	○
3. There is a new teacher at Adams Elementary.		○	○	○	○
4. There is a teacher at Adams Elementary named Mr. Tanner.		○	○	○	○

Part 2: Fill in the bubble next to the best answer to each question.

5. Which of the sources is written in a first-person voice?

Ⓐ Source 1

Ⓑ Source 2

Ⓒ Source 3

Ⓓ Source 4

6. Which two words from Source 4 are homophones?

Ⓐ *sighed* and *sight*

Ⓑ *knew* and *know*

Ⓒ *knew* and *new*

Ⓓ *retrieve* and *find*

7. Which set of words is used as synonyms in the sources? (The source number is given in parentheses. Be careful: The words must be used as synonyms in the same source.)

Ⓐ *evaporate* (2) and *condense* (2)

Ⓑ *illustrated* (3) and *drawn* (3)

Ⓒ *artwork* (3) and *visuals* (3)

Ⓓ *used* (2) and *reused* (2)

8. Which of the following quotes from the sources describes something that is easily found if one knows where to look for it?

Ⓐ "pull the missing data out of thin air"

Ⓑ "hiding in plain sight"

Ⓒ "a split-second decision"

Ⓓ "Technology is another story."

Part 3: Search "Into and Out of Thin Air" to find examples of adverbs with the following meanings. Then write the number of the source in which you located this information.

9. "done with great care" _____ Source #: _____

10. "happening by accident" _____ Source #: _____

Into and Out of Thin Air *(cont.)*

Name: _____

Part 4: Refer back to the sources to answer these questions.

11. Imagine that you are one of Mr. Tanner's students. It is your assignment to illustrate the water cycle. You must use the information given in Source 2 to do this.

Draw the water cycle below, and label each of the four steps. Be sure to include the following things in your illustration: **rain, cloud, lake, land, water vapor**.

Name: _____

Part 4 *(cont.):* Refer back to the sources, and use complete sentences to answer these questions.

12. When water is heated, it turns into a gas, evaporates, and rises up to the sky. Does it vanish into thin air? Use the information from the sources to explain your answer.

_____

_____

_____

_____

_____

13. Rewrite Mr. Tanner's experience from Source 3, but use a first-person voice. Write about the experience as if you are Mr. Tanner.

_____

_____

_____

_____

_____

_____

_____

_____

_____

_____

_____

Now answer this question: In your opinion, which voice (first person or third person) is a more effective choice for this type of story? Why?

_____

_____

_____

Additional Activities

1. Now that you have read all of the sources for this unit, do you see any connections between them? What do they have in common? Write up to four connections. (Note: Some units may have fewer.)

_____   _____

_____   _____

Now go back and rank the connections you have just written. Which one seems to be the strongest or most important to the overall unit? Write a "1" next to the strongest connection, a "2" next to the second-strongest, etc.

2. Fill in the chart below to show the elements that describe each source. You may fill in as many bubbles as are appropriate. (Note: Some rows will be left blank if there are fewer than four sources in the unit.)

Source # Element ➡	fiction	nonfiction	chart	map	graph	diagram
Source 1	◯	◯	◯	◯	◯	◯
Source 2	◯	◯	◯	◯	◯	◯
Source 3	◯	◯	◯	◯	◯	◯
Source 4	◯	◯	◯	◯	◯	◯

3. It's your turn to be a teacher. Write a new multiple-choice question based on the reading sources. Then provide four answer choices, only one of which is correct. If possible, make your "students" dig a little deeper to find the correct answer to your question. Don't make your question one whose answer is written directly in the text.

Your Question: _____

_____

Ⓐ _____   Ⓒ _____

Ⓑ _____   Ⓓ _____

4. Once again, imagine that you are the teacher. Think of two words, phrases, numbers, etc., that your students will need to search the sources to find. For example, give the definition of a word, and have everyone find that word. Name a part of speech and ask for an example. Challenge your "students" to find a word with a certain number of syllables. There are many possibilities.

Search for _____

Search for _____

Answer Key

Unit 1. Creating a Stir (page 6)
Part 1
1. Source 2
2. Sources 2 and 3
3. Source 2
4. Sources 2 and 3

Part 2
5. B and C 6. B and D 7. A 8. B

Part 3
The source number is given in parentheses.
9. Rumble! (3), Scrape! (3), Clang! (3)
10. It's like living inside a washing machine. (3); They will stick out like a sore thumb. (3)

Part 4
11. "The whispering whir of the windmills will soon signal a new era of energy efficiency." (Source 2)

12.

	Source 2	Source 3
Pollution	Wind energy is clean. It doesn't pollute the air, land, or water like fossil fuels do.	Wind energy causes noise pollution. The constant sounds of the windmill's blades and of the air moving are loud and disturbing.
Cost	Wind is free. While wind farms cost money to build, that money is made back in the end.	It costs millions to build wind farms. There is nothing free about them.
Freedom	Using wind energy will free us from giving our money to other countries for their fossil fuels.	By relying on the weather, we will lose the freedom we have of simply flipping a switch to get electricity.

13. In a literal sense, windmills stir the air because they have moving blades. These blades move the air, and this is how energy is created. In a figurative sense, the issue of whether or not to build wind farms is creating a stir because it is controversial. Not everyone agrees that it's a good idea.

Unit 2. Falling Off and Growing In (page 9)
Part 1
1. Sources 3 and 4
2. Sources 3 and 4
3. Sources 1 and 2
4. Source 2

Part 2
5. B 6. D 7. C 8. A

Part 3
The source number is given in parentheses.
9. uproar (3) 10. emerge (4)

Part 4
11. Student sketches should show two trees. The tree on the left should be labeled *coniferous*. It should grow upward, have needles instead of leaves, and be triangular in shape. The tree on the right should be labeled *deciduous*. It should grow outward and have leaves (or it could be bare, as if the leaves have fallen off).

12. The narrator is most likely between the ages of 13 and 17. We know from Source 3 that he has 28 permanent teeth. We know from Source 4 that a child loses his/her primary teeth by age 13 but doesn't grow the final four permanent teeth until around age 17 at the earliest.

13. Two other terms for "baby teeth" are "primary teeth" and "deciduous teeth." The term "primary teeth" is explicitly given in Sources 3 and 4. The term "deciduous teeth" can be inferred. We know from Source 1 that humans have "deciduous teeth" (teeth that fall out as the human develops). This process is dramatized in Source 3, where the narrator refers to a "long word" for the sister's baby teeth. From the clues given, we can infer that this long word is *deciduous*.

Unit 3. The Dynamic Trio (page 12)
Part 1
1. Sources 2 and 4
2. Sources 2 and 4
3. Source 2
4. Sources 2 and 3

Part 2
5. B 6. D 7. C 8. C

Part 3
The source number is given in parentheses.
9. dreadful (4) 10. vie (2)

Part 4
11. Accept appropriate responses. Students may write that Rico is the practical or organized one who asks questions and makes sure the group has a plan. Carmen is the agreeable one who is friendly and is easygoing. Carl is the picky one who has strong opinions.

12. Carmen: must be home by 10 p.m.; Carl: won't see movies about kids or animals, won't see a science-fiction sequel; Rico: can't go out until after 6 p.m., won't see *Old Hat*

13.

Answer Key (cont.)

Unit 4. #Symbols (page 16)

Part 1

1. Sources 2 and 3
2. Source 2
3. Sources 1 and 2
4. Source 2

Part 2

5. D   6. C   7. C   8. B

Part 3

The source number is given in parentheses.

9. That's (3)   10. 1700s (3)

Part 4

11. Accept appropriate responses. For the positives, students may say that symbols are shorter to write than words, and whole groups of people understand what a symbol means (as in the case of the dollar sign on the thief's bag in Source 1). For the negatives, students may point out that some symbols have more than one meaning and this can be confusing (as in the case of the # sign) or possibly even dangerous (as is the claim of the author in Source 3).

12. Accept appropriate summaries that briefly describe the aunt's issue in Source 3 with the use of the skull-and-crossbones label on the poisonous products (children are drawn to this symbol because it is also the symbol for pirate ships, and many children like the cartoon versions of pirates they see on TV).

13. Accept appropriate responses that take a consistent position and provide reasoning for that position.

Unit 5. The Prototype (page 19)

Part 1

1. Sources 1, 2, and 4
2. Source 4
3. Sources 3 and 4
4. Source 3

Part 2

5. A   6. C   7. B   8. B and D

Part 3

The source number is given in parentheses.

9. cushiony (3)   10. detachable (3)

Part 4

11. Students should write and draw the following:
Station 1: Gary, circle on top of square; Station 2: Lucy, pentagon on circle on top of square; Station 3: Kerry, ovals added on either side of figure from Station 2; Station 4: Keith, rectangles added to bottom of figure from Station 3; Station 5: Stan, triangle on top of figure from Station 4; Station 6: Leeland, a large box with a shipping label

12. Using the new method, Ford's factory built **4** complete Model T cars in 12 hours. This left them with **2** hours left over to begin building a **5th** car.

13. Accept appropriate answers. Students might mention the name of the doll's creator (Leeland Lewis) and the story of how the doll was first produced in his parents' garage. Students should correctly incorporate at least three of the terms from Source 2.

Unit 6. A Little from a Lot (page 22)

Part 1

1. 10,000   2. 4,000   3. 100   4. $20,000

Part 2

5. B   6. C   7. B   8. B and C

Part 3

The source number is given in parentheses.

9. guesstimate (4)   10. fantabulous (4)

Part 4

11. Students could possibly make a case for A or B, but the best answer is C. Crowdfunding could be summed up by the words "a little from a lot" because a little bit of money is donated by a lot of people. These donations add up and make it possible for a business venture to succeed.

12. Accept appropriate responses. Students should write a paragraph that flows well and contains all of the important pieces of information about crowdfunding.

13. Accept appropriate responses. Students should draw pictures that correspond to the incentives offered in Source 4 (e.g., musical notes or a digital music player for the first incentive, a picture of the doll for the second, etc.).

Unit 7. A Fit for Her Environment (page 26)

Part 1

1. Sources 3 and 4
2. Source 3
3. Source 1
4. Sources 2 and 4

Part 2

5. B   6. D   7. D   8. B

Part 3

The source number is given in parentheses.

9. drenched (1), sweaty (1)
10. enlarged (4), extra-large (4)

Part 4

11. The term "coolest" can refer to temperature, or it can refer to something that is preferable. Ann might have found the black shirt to be preferable in a fashion sense, but it was the exact opposite when it came to the temperature.

12. The black lines should be drawn under the player's eyes. The black lines (on both the player and the cheetah) attract the light of the sun, thus keeping it out of the eyes. This would help a person or animal see better on a sunny day.

Answer Key *(cont.)*

13. From Source 2, we learn that grasslands have hot summers, wide-open spaces, and they are the home to grazing animals. From Source 1, we learn that black attracts the light of the sun. From Source 4, we learn that cheetahs have black tear marks near their eyes, which help them see better in sunny conditions. We also learn that their bodies help them use oxygen well, which helps them run. In addition, we learn that they hunt animals like antelopes and zebras. From Source 3, we learn that cheetahs are much faster than antelopes and zebras, which are two of their main sources of food.

Unit 8. The Early Shift *(page 29)*

Part 1
1. Source 4
2. Sources 1, 3, and 4
3. Sources 1 and 3
4. Source 3

Part 2
5. B   6. A   7. C   8. D

Part 3
The source number is given in parentheses.
9. ASAP (4)   10. ice-cold (4)

Part 4
11.

Source #	Narrator	Example of Hyperbole
1	Sammy	"Seth is my older brother, so I know for a fact that he's the laziest person on the planet."
3	Seth's mom	"I've done the math in my head a million times, and I hope Seth has done it, too."
4	Seth	"The clock says '4:44', which obviously is too early for the human brain to function properly."

12. He did give himself enough time. According to Source 2, Hardy's Hardware opens at 7:00 a.m. on Saturday. According to Source 3, Mr. Hardy wants Seth to be there an hour early, so by 6:00 a.m. Seth woke up at 4:44 a.m. According to Seth's mom, it will take Seth 45 minutes to get ready and 15 minutes to drive to Hardy's. That equals one hour, which should get him to the store by about 5:45 a.m.
13. Accept appropriate responses that establish a plausible voice for Mr. Hardy.

Unit 9. The Golden Door *(page 32)*

Part 1
1. Source 3
2. Sources 2 and 3
3. Sources 1 and 2
4. Source 1

Part 2
5. D   6. C   7. B   8. B

Part 3
The source number is given in parentheses.
9. 1883 (2), 1886 (2), 1899 (1)
10. permanently (3)

Part 4
11. Accept appropriate responses.
12. An appropriate answer might mention the following: the Statue of Liberty holds a torch/lamp up high; she sits on Liberty Island, which is just south of Ellis Island; immigrants passed by her on their way to a new life in America.
13. 1. Lower Bay, 2. The Narrows, 3. Upper Bay, 4. Liberty Island, 5. Ellis Island, 6. Manhattan

Unit 10. The Impossible Dream *(page 36)*

Part 1
1. Source 3
2. Sources 1 and 3
3. Sources 2 and 3
4. Sources 2 and 3

Part 2
5. C   6. C   7. A   8. B

Part 3
The source number is given in parentheses.
9. recognizable (3)   10. emphatically (2)

Part 4
11. Answers can be given in either order.

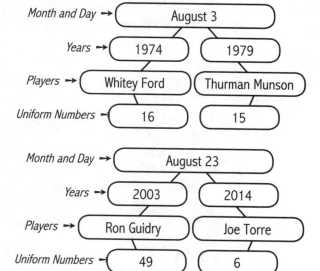

Month and Day →	August 3	
Years →	1974	1979
Players →	Whitey Ford	Thurman Munson
Uniform Numbers →	16	15
Month and Day →	August 23	
Years →	2003	2014
Players →	Ron Guidry	Joe Torre
Uniform Numbers →	49	6

12. This statement is true. Source 1 tells us that only players who were currently wearing #42 prior to April 15, 1997, were allowed to continue doing so. It also tells us that only one player continued wearing the number on a regular basis after 2004. The question tells us that Rivera retired from the Yankees in 2013, which implies that he was that one player.

13.

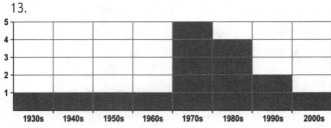

   A. 1970s
   B. 2. There were 16 numbers retired during these 8 decades. $16 \div 8 = 2$
   C. 25%. Four of the 16 numbers were retired during the 1980s. $\frac{4}{16} = \frac{1}{4} = 25\%$
   D. Accept appropriate questions that can be answered by information given in the graph. Students should include one correct answer and three incorrect answers, as well.

Unit 11. Selling Snacks (page 41)

Part 1

1. Sources 1 and 3   3. Source 1
2. Source 3   4. Sources 2 and 3

Part 2

5. B   6. A   7. C   8. D

Part 3

The source number is given in parentheses.

9. estimate (3)   10. upcoming (3)

Part 4

11. what it costs to produce each package
   A. $4.09 − $2.84 = $1.25
   B. $2.99 − $1.49 = $1.50
   C. $4.29 − $2.29 = $2.00
   D. $3.59 − $1.79 = $1.80
   E. $2.29 − $0.89 = $1.40

12. ×
   A. $1.25 × 1,200 = $1,500
   B. $1.50 × 960 = $1,440
   C. $2.00 × 750 = $1,500
   D. $1.80 × 900 = $1,620
   E. $1.40 × 1,000 = $1,400

13. A. Kale Crunchies

B. Walnutty Wafers
C. Blueberry Blasts and Chia Squares
D. The bar graph best illustrates the data. The profits for each snack are very similar. In the pie chart, all of the sections seem to be about the same size, which does not give a clear picture of which snacks earn more profit. In the bar graph, it is much easier to compare the different profit earnings for each snack.

Unit 12. In More Than One Place (page 46)

Part 1

1. Source 2   3. Source 3
2. Sources 2 and 3   4. Source 1

Part 2

5. A   6. D   7. C   8. C

Part 3

The source number is given in parentheses.

9. International (2)   10. blurted (1)

Part 4

11.

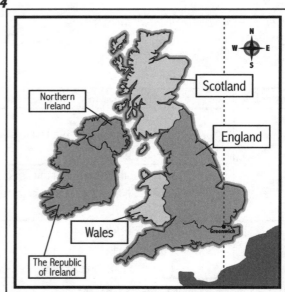

Ireland is located entirely within the <u>Western</u> Hemisphere.

12. **The British Isles:** Dublin, England, Greenwich, London, Northern Ireland, The Republic of Ireland, Scotland, Wales
Great Britain: England, Greenwich, London, Scotland, Wales
Ireland: Dublin, Northern Ireland, The Republic of Ireland
United Kingdom: England, Greenwich, London, Northern Ireland, Scotland, Wales

13. This title fits this collection of sources in several ways. First, the place that the main character (Matt) is visiting can go by many names. While he is in London, he could

say that he is in the British Isles, the United Kingdom, Great Britain, etc. Then, when he puts one foot on either side of the Prime Meridian marking in Greenwich, he is in both of Earth's hemispheres at the same time. Students could also mention that at the end of his email, Matt says even though he is thousands of miles away, his thoughts are with his family back home. In a figurative sense, this puts him in more than one place at one time.

Unit 13. More Rare Than Gold (page 50)

Part 1
1. Source 1
2. Sources 1 and 2
3. Source 2
4. Sources 2 and 3

Part 2
5. B
6. C and D
7. A
8. B

Part 3
The source number is given in parentheses.
9. recently concluded (1)
10. deemed inferior (3)

Part 4
11. Accept appropriate responses. The following is just an example. Other answers may be correct.

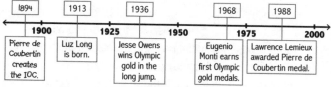

12. Instead of using the word *help*, the writer uses forms of the words *aid*, *assist*, etc. Accept appropriate responses to the final part of the question.
13. Accept appropriate responses. A well-written response will point out specific similarities and differences between the two athletes' stories. Similarities: Both helped their competitors. Both put sportsmanship above their desires to win. Both lost gold medals as a result of their acts of sportsmanship. Differences: Long competed in the Summer Olympic Games, while Monti competed in the Winter Olympic Games. Long only competed in one Olympic Games, while Monti competed in three. Unlike Monti, he never earned a gold medal. Long's act was courageous because of his leader's beliefs.

Unit 14. Around a Long Time (page 54)

Part 1
1. Source 1
2. Sources 1 and 3
3. Sources 1 and 3
4. Sources 1 and 3

Part 2
5. B and D
6. A and B
7. B
8. A and D

Part 3
The source number is given in parentheses.
9. paronomasia (2)
10. humorous (2)

Part 4
11. B — to look at his website. This is a pun because it uses the fact that there are websites (pages to visit) on a computer, while spiders also make webs at a site (place) in nature.
12. *Setup:* I can see why this *yong* character means 'eternity.'
    Punchline: It would take me a really *yong* time to learn how to do it correctly.
    Why It's a Pun: She's using the word *yong* (the name of the character she's trying to write) as a substitute for the word *long*. This works because *yong* means "forever," and forever is a very long time.
13. Accept appropriate responses. The stroke name and number should match, and the student should use his/her own words to describe how the stroke is written.

Unit 15. Six Honest Serving-Men (page 58)

Part 1
1. Paragraph 3
2. Paragraphs 1 and 3
3. Paragraph 2
4. Paragraphs 1 and 3

Part 2
5. B
6. C
7. A
8. B

Part 3
9. Wildcats Suffer First Loss (3)
10. by Aurora Lee (3)

Part 4
11. Scoreboard 1 is correct. It accurately shows that the Wildcats scored a run in the top of the first inning, and the Hornets scored four runs in the bottom of the sixth inning. Scoreboard 2 shows the runs being scored in different innings.
12. Another name would be the 5 Ws and an H. These six elements are important because they tell the reader what he or she needs to know about the subject of the article.
13. Accept appropriate responses that categorize the information as very important, supporting, or least important to the main idea of the article.
    1. A, 2. C, 3. B, 4. A, 5. B, 6. A

Unit 16. A Cache of Cash on Cache (page 62)

Part 1
1. Sources 1 and 3
2. Source 3
3. Sources 1 and 3
4. Source 4

Part 2
5. B
6. A and D
7. C
8. C

Part 3

The source number is given in parentheses.

9. quartet (3)   10. fluttered (1)

Part 4

11. From Source 2, we know that the word *cache* means "a hidden supply of something." Therefore, it makes sense that a hidden treasure would be located on a street with that name.

12.

	Clue #1	Clue #2	Clue #3	Clue #4
Where was it located?	doghouse	clock	tree	grill
Which letter was there?	S	A	N	D

13. A. It is located in the sandbox.
    B. After visiting all of the locations, you will collect the letters S, A, N, and D. These spell *sand*. The writer of Source 3 tells us that will be the location of the treasure.
    C. $547.60
    D. Put the numbers four, five, six, and seven in alphabetical order; then put a decimal point to the left of the final number.

Unit 17. Seeing Eye to Eye (page 66)

Part 1

1. Cory and Rory   3. Tori
2. Cory, Rory, and Tony   4. Rory and Tony

Part 2

5. A and C   6. D   7. C   8. A

Part 3

The source number is given in parentheses.

9. toxic (3)   10. aggressive (3)

Part 4

11. ƎƆИA⅃UᙠMA

12. This statement could not literally be true because if one looked into a mirror, one would see a reverse image. This is why the word AMBULANCE is written backwards on emergency vehicles. If Cory and Rory are identical in appearance, then looking at each other would not be looking in a mirror. They would not see the reverse of each other's appearance. In the mirror version, the hair would be parted to the left, for example, and the right ear would be larger than the left.

13. The expression "don't see eye to eye" is an idiom, as explained in Source 1. It means that the two don't agree on many things. In this case, this expression is also an example of irony because these two people are identical twins. Therefore, they are almost exactly the same physically (same height, etc.) and would literally be able to see eye to eye better than most other sets of people.

Unit 18. All Ears (page 69)

Part 1

1. Source 1   3. Source 1
2. Sources 1 and 3   4. Sources 2 and 3

Part 2

5. A and B   6. C   7. A   8. D

Part 3

The source number is given in parentheses.

9. unearthed (1)   10. unearthed (1)

Part 4

11. The main character from Source 1 is most likely familiar with the information given in Source 2. We know this because the character thinks back to first reading about the planet Polypinnae in school. Also, Source 2 mentions that the planet is named after the creatures who live there. We learn from Source 2 that this name means "many wings" or "many ears." In Source 1, the character says, "I knew from their planet's name that they would have many ears."

12. Accept reasonable responses. Students should show four scenes that summarize the events of Source 1. For example: Panel 1 could show the protagonist speaking into his/her megaphone with the spacecraft in the background, Panel 2 could show the Polypin telling him/her to quiet down, Panel 3 could show the protagonist telling them about the threat, and Panel 4 could show them not paying attention to his/her words.

13. The Polypins are ironic because they appear to be all ears, but they are not good listeners. This is ironic because the idiom "all ears" is used to describe someone who is intently listening—something the Polypins don't seem to be interested in doing.

Unit 19. All Thumbs (page 72)

Part 1

1. QWERTY and KALQ   3. KALQ
2. QWERTY and KALQ   4. QWERTY and KALQ

Part 2

5. D   6. A   7. D   8. B

Part 3

The source number is given in parentheses.

9. downloaded (4)   10. throwback (4)

Answer Key (cont.)

Part 4

11. He means that it is old and no longer a part of today's world. It is a metaphor because dinosaurs and computer keyboards have little in common; the word *dinosaur* is only used to illustrate how out-of-date Charley feels the keyboard is.

12. Accept appropriate responses in which the student chooses a position and give reasons to support it.

13. The central idea is that the blogger is as much a user of today's technology as anyone, but the way she learned how to type (on a large keyboard) is not very useful anymore. Students should cite details that show how the world in which the blogger lives is different from the world of the past where all typing was done in a seated position in front of a desktop typewriter or keyboard.

Unit 20. All the Same to Me (page 76)

Part 1

1. Source 3
2. Sources 1 and 3
3. Sources 1 and 3
4. Source 1

Part 2

5. A   6. A   7. B   8. D

Part 3

The source number is given in parentheses.

9. short-term jobs (2)   10. win-win situation (1)

Part 4

11. The insect pictured is an ant. In Source 2, we learn that, unlike a termite, an ant has bent antennae. We also learn that its body narrows a lot between the thorax and the abdomen. Both of these characteristics can be seen in the picture.

12. Students should use evidence from Sources 1 and 3 in their answers. Some characteristics that should be mentioned include the following (with the source number noted in parentheses): length of tongue (1, 3); narrowness of tongue (1, 3); presence of spines (1); presence of extra saliva (1); speed at which the tongue can be flicked (3).

13. Accept appropriate responses.

Unit 21. Not the Same Thing (page 79)

Part 1

1. Sources 1 and 2
2. Source 2
3. Source 1
4. Source 3

Part 2

5. B   6. A   7. C   8. B

Part 3

The source number is given in parentheses.

9. cupboards (2), homemade (2), teaspoon (3)

10. buttermilk (2), tablespoon (3)

Part 4

11. You can mix 8 teaspoons of cream of tartar with 4 teaspoons of baking soda to get 12 teaspoons of baking powder. In Source 2, we are told that baking powder can be made by mixing 2 parts cream of tartar with 1 part baking soda. That means that $\frac{2}{3}$ of the mixture will be cream of tartar and $\frac{1}{3}$ will be baking soda. Two-thirds of 12 teaspoons is 8 teaspoons, and $\frac{1}{3}$ equals 4 teaspoons.

12. Her mother's recipe was to blame. The ingredients in the recipe aren't acidic enough, so baking powder was needed. Mia's mother recited the recipe from memory, and she mistakenly wrote down "baking soda" instead of "baking powder." This meant that not enough gas bubbles were released into the dough, so it didn't rise properly.

13. Baking soda is a basic substance, and vinegar is an acidic substance. When they are combined, a chemical reaction occurs. Bubbles of carbon dioxide gas form and begin to rise. Because this substance occurs inside a model volcano, it has nowhere to go but up and out of the volcano.

Unit 22. Chasing the Cheese (page 82)

Part 1

1. Sources 1 and 4
2. Sources 2, 3, and 4
3. Sources 3 and 4
4. Sources 1, 3, and 4

Part 2

5. B   6. B   7. C   8. A

Part 3

The source number is given in parentheses.

9. Cooper's (2, 3, 4), Allison's (2)
10. genuinely (2), impossibly (4)

Part 4

11. Source 1 and Source 2 are both written to people the authors care about. Source 1 is written from a daughter to her mother. The tone of this e-mail is excitement. The author focuses on the tradition of the event and how it might become a tradition for her family, too. Source 2 is written from a mother to her daughter. The tone of this e-mail is concern. The author focuses on the dangers of the event. She includes a photo of the hill to drive home her point that it is too steep to run down.

12. Paragraph 1 begins with a question. It asks the reader think about competing in the contest. Paragraph 2 begins by introducing two specific contestants. It goes on to give us some background about these people. Paragraph 3 begins by describing the hill. It gives us more details about the race itself. Paragraph 4 begins

Answer Key (cont.)

by telling us which contestant was injured. It goes on to detail her injuries. Paragraph 5 begins by telling us that one of contestants did succeed. It goes on to tell us more about the experience of winning the race. The purpose of the sidebar is to quickly give us some facts about the contest.

13. Accept appropriate responses that follow the structure outlined in the directions on the page.

Unit 23. Two Singular Creatures (page 87)
Part 1
1. Sources 1 and 2
2. Sources 2, 3, and 4
3. Sources 2 and 3
4. Source 3

Part 2
5. D   6. B   7. B   8. C

Part 3
The source number is given in parentheses.
9. inches (3), pouches (4)   10. children (3), teeth (4)

Part 4
11. Accept appropriate responses. Students might say that Source 3 contains a sidebar, whereas Source 4 does not. They also might say that Source 3 immediately names the subject of the report (star-nosed mole), whereas Source 4 does not reveal the subject (platypus) until the end of the report.
12. Accept appropriate responses that include the three definitions of *singular* provided in Source 1.
13. Accept appropriate responses in which students draw and label a hybrid animal in the box and describe that animal on the lines below the box.

Unit 24. Appropriately Named (page 92)
Part 1
Accept appropriate responses. Possible answers include:
1. mini, miniature, miniscule
2. rare
3. shining, spotless, stainless
4. unusual, unfamiliar; usual, uninteresting, unimaginative

Part 2
5. A   6. B   7. C   8. C

Part 3
The source number is given in parentheses.
9. jangling (1), crinkling (1)
10. scientifically (3)

Part 4
11. Accept reasonable responses. Students may write that "Eva and Evan's Difficult and Diurnal Word Tournament" is appropriately named because it is very challenging and it takes place each day.
12. Accept reasonable responses. Students may write that *Ephemeroptera* is an appropriate name for the mayfly because of the meaning of the two Greek roots that form the word. *Ephemeros* means "short lived," and adult mayflies don't live for very long. *Pteron* means "wing," and only the adults have wings. This means that when you see a mayfly with wings, it does not have long to live.
13. Accept reasonable responses. Students may write that Evan likes words, so he would be most interested in the way the word *Ephemeroptera* is formed and the meaning of its Greek roots. He would also likely be interested in the information in the sidebar, which explains the meaning of the word *vestigial*.

Unit 25. Into and Out of Thin Air (page 96)
Part 1
1. Source 2
2. Sources 2 and 3
3. Sources 3 and 4
4. Sources 2 and 3

Part 2
5. D   6. C   7. C   8. B

Part 3
The source number is given in parentheses.
9. painstakingly (3)   10. unintentionally (4)

Part 4
11. Students should illustrate the water cycle according to the descriptions given in Source 2. In addition, students should include the elements mentioned in the question and label each of the four stages (evaporation, condensation, precipitation, and collection) on their illustrations.
12. Accept appropriate answers. Students should say that the water doesn't vanish into thin air. If it vanished into thin air, the water would disappear completely, never to return. That is not how the water cycle works. Instead, the water eventually cools down, returns to liquid form, and becomes clouds.
13. Student writing should follow the basic storyline of Source 3 but should be written in first-person. Accept appropriate responses for the follow-up question. Students should state an opinion and provide reasoning for that opinion.

Common Core State Standards

The lessons and activities included in *Mastering Complex Text Using Multiple Reading Sources, Grade 6* meet the following Common Core State Standards. (©Copyright 2010. National Governors Association Center for Best Practices and Council of Chief State School Officers. All rights reserved.) For more information about the Common Core State Standards, go to *http://www.corestandards.org/* or visit *http://www.teachercreated.com/standards/* for more correlations to Common Core State Standards.

Reading: Informational Text	
Key Ideas and Details	**Units**
ELA.RI.6.1 Cite textual evidence to support analysis of what the text says explicitly as well as inferences drawn from the text.	1–25
ELA.RI.6.2 Determine a central idea of a text and how it is conveyed through particular details; provide a summary of the text distinct from personal opinions or judgments.	1, 3–4, 6–7, 9–10, 12–13, 15–19, 21–25
ELA.RI.6.3 Analyze in detail how a key individual, event, or idea is introduced, illustrated, and elaborated in a text (e.g., through examples or anecdotes).	1–25
Craft and Structure	**Units**
ELA.RI.6.4 Determine the meaning of words and phrases as they are used in a text, including figurative, connotative, and technical meanings.	1–25
ELA.RI.6.5 Analyze how a particular sentence, paragraph, chapter, or section fits into the overall structure of a text and contributes to the development of the ideas.	1–25
ELA.RI.6.6 Determine an author's point of view or purpose in a text and explain how it is conveyed in the text.	1, 4, 6–8, 14, 17–20, 22–25
Integration of Knowledge and Ideas	**Units**
ELA.RI.6.7 Integrate information presented in different media or formats (e.g., visually, quantitatively) as well as in words to develop a coherent understanding of a topic or issue.	1–25
ELA.RI.6.8 Trace and evaluate the argument and specific claims in a text, distinguishing claims that are supported by reasons and evidence from claims that are not.	1, 4, 6, 8, 17, 22–23
ELA.RI.6.9 Compare and contrast one author's presentation of events with that of another (e.g., a memoir written by and a biography on the same person).	1, 8, 13, 22–23
Range of Reading and Level of Text Complexity	**Units**
ELA.RI.6.10 By the end of the year, read and comprehend literary nonfiction in the grades 6–8 text complexity band proficiently, with scaffolding as needed at the high end of the range.	1–25

Common Core State Standards *(cont.)*

Reading: Literature	
Key Ideas and Details	**Units**
ELA.RL.6.1 Cite textual evidence to support analysis of what the text says explicitly as well as inferences drawn from the text.	1–25
ELA.RL.6.2 Determine a theme or central idea of a text and how it is conveyed through particular details; provide a summary of the text distinct from personal opinions or judgments.	1, 3–4, 6–7, 9–10, 12–13, 15–19, 21–25
ELA.RL.6.3 Describe how a particular story's or drama's plot unfolds in a series of episodes as well as how the characters respond or change as the plot moves toward a resolution.	3, 8, 12–13, 18, 24–25
Craft and Structure	**Units**
ELA.RL.6.4 Determine the meaning of words and phrases as they are used in a text, including figurative and connotative meanings; analyze the impact of a specific word choice on meaning and tone.	1–25
ELA.RL.6.5 Analyze how a particular sentence, chapter, scene, or stanza fits into the overall structure of a text and contributes to the development of the theme, setting, or plot.	1–25
ELA.RL.6.6 Explain how an author develops the point of view of the narrator or speaker in a text.	1–4, 8–10, 17–19, 22–25
Integration of Knowledge and Ideas	**Units**
ELA.RL.6.9 Compare and contrast texts in different forms or genres (e.g., stories and poems; historical novels and fantasy stories) in terms of their approaches to similar themes and topics.	6, 9–11, 18, 23, 25
Range of Reading and Level of Text Complexity	**Units**
ELA.RL.6.10 By the end of the year, read and comprehend literature, including stories, dramas, and poems, in the grades 6–8 text complexity band proficiently, with scaffolding as needed at the high end of the range.	1–25

Common Core State Standards *(cont.)*

Writing	
Text Types and Purposes	**Units**
ELA.W.6.1 Write arguments to support claims with clear reasons and relevant evidence.	1–25
ELA.W.6.1A Introduce claim(s) and organize the reasons and evidence clearly.	1–25
ELA.W.6.1B Support claim(s) with clear reasons and relevant evidence, using credible sources and demonstrating an understanding of the topic or text.	1–25
ELA.W.6.1C Use words, phrases, and clauses to clarify the relationships among claim(s) and reasons.	1–25
ELA.W.6.2 Write informative/explanatory texts to examine a topic and convey ideas, concepts, and information through the selection, organization, and analysis of relevant content.	1–25
ELA.W.6.2A Introduce a topic; organize ideas, concepts, and information, using strategies such as definition, classification, comparison/contrast, and cause/effect; include formatting (e.g., headings), graphics (e.g., charts, tables), and multimedia when useful to aiding comprehension.	1–25
ELA.W.6.2B Develop the topic with relevant facts, definitions, concrete details, quotations, or other information and examples.	1–25
ELA.W.6.2D Use precise language and domain-specific vocabulary to inform about or explain the topic.	1–25
ELA.W.6.3 Write narratives to develop real or imagined experiences or events using effective technique, descriptive details, and clear event sequences.	4–6, 8–10, 13, 19–21, 23–25
Production and Distribution of Writing	**Units**
ELA.W.6.4 Produce clear and coherent writing in which the development and organization are appropriate to task, purpose, and audience.	1–25
Research to Build and Present Knowledge	**Units**
ELA.W.6.8 Gather relevant information from multiple print and digital sources; assess the credibility of each source; and quote or paraphrase the data and conclusions of others while avoiding plagiarism and providing basic bibliographic information for sources.	1–25
ELA.W.6.9 Draw evidence from literary or informational texts to support analysis, reflection, and research.	1–25
Range of Writing	**Units**
ELA.W.6.10 Write routinely over extended time frames (time for research, reflection, and revision) and shorter time frames (a single sitting or a day or two) for a range of discipline-specific tasks, purposes, and audiences.	1–25

Common Core State Standards *(cont.)*

Language	
Conventions of Standard English	**Units**
ELA.L.6.1 Demonstrate command of the conventions of standard English grammar and usage when writing or speaking.	1–25
ELA.L.6.2 Demonstrate command of the conventions of standard English capitalization, punctuation, and spelling when writing.	1–25
Knowledge of Language	**Units**
ELA.L.6.3 Use knowledge of language and its conventions when writing, speaking, reading, or listening.	1–25
Vocabulary Acquisition and Use	**Units**
ELA.L.6.4 Determine or clarify the meaning of unknown and multiple-meaning words and phrases based on grade 6 reading and content, choosing flexibly from a range of strategies.	1–25
ELA.L.6.4A Use context (e.g., the overall meaning of a sentence or paragraph; a word's position or function in a sentence) as a clue to the meaning of a word or phrase.	1–25
ELA.L.6.4B Use common, grade-appropriate Greek or Latin affixes and roots as clues to the meaning of a word (e.g., *audience, auditory, audible*).	18, 24
ELA.L.6.5 Demonstrate understanding of figurative language, word relationships, and nuances in word meanings.	1–25
ELA.L.6.5A Interpret figures of speech (e.g., personification) in context.	1–2, 6–9, 14–15, 17–19, 21–22, 25
ELA.L.6.5B Use the relationship between particular words (e.g., cause/effect, part/whole, item/category) to better understand each of the words.	1–25
ELA.L.6.5C Distinguish among the connotations (associations) of words with similar denotations (definitions) (e.g., *stingy, scrimping, economical, unwasteful, thrifty*).	1–4, 8–9, 14, 17, 21–22, 24
ELA.L.6.6 Acquire and use accurately grade-appropriate general academic and domain-specific words and phrases; gather vocabulary knowledge when considering a word or phrase important to comprehension or expression.	1–25